MORE THAN A
PINK
CADILLAC

More Than a Pink Cadillac is a how-to manual for business and life.

With faith in God and old-fashioned values, Mary Kay Ash built one of America's most admired companies. She turned a $5,000 investment into a billion-dollar corporation and along the way helped thousands of women launch successful careers.

This book is filled with inspirational tales of modest women with grand expectations. Their stories are proof that success is based on choices, not circumstances.

In an era when profit making dominates the headlines, finding a business that emphasizes people is a simple delight. Great leaders—be they generals, chief executive officers, teachers, or parents—understand the value of personal relationships. Mary Kay was devoted to her sales force and employees and expected the best from them—and they gave her their best. This was the basis of their personal success and the success of Mary Kay Cosmetics.

–Kay Bailey Hutchison
United States Senate

MORE THAN A PINK CADILLAC

Mary Kay Inc.'s
Nine Leadership Keys to Success

JIM UNDERWOOD

McGRAW-HILL

NEW YORK   CHICAGO   SAN FRANCISCO   LISBON
LONDON   MADRID   MEXICO CITY   MILAN   NEW DELHI
SAN JUAN   SEOUL   SINGAPORE   SYDNEY   TORONTO

The *McGraw·Hill* Companies

4 5 6 7 8 9 0   DOC/DOC   0 9 8 7 6 5 4 3

ISBN 0-07-140839-8

McGraw-Hill books are available at special discounts to use as premiums and sales promotions, or for use in corporate training programs. For more information, please write to the Director of Special Sales, Professional Publishing, McGraw-Hill, Two Penn Plaza, New York, NY 10121-2298. Or contact your local bookstore.

Library of Congress Cataloging-in-Publication Data
Underwood, Jim, 1941–
   More than a pink Cadillac / by Jim Underwood.
      p. cm.
   Includes index.
    ISBN 0-07-140839-8 (Hardcover : alk. paper)
    1. Leadership.   2. Success in business.   3. Mary Kay Cosmetics—Case studies.
   I. Title.
   HD57.7 .U527 2002
   658.4'092—dc21
                                    2002152472

Contents

Acknowledgments

This book is dedicated to Mary Kay Ash. When she left this world in November 2001, it was not the same place it had been when she arrived. Through her principles, inspiration, and leadership, the lives of tens of thousands of people around the world have been changed for the better. Truly, she was one of the best chief executive officers who ever led a company.

I want to thank the members of the Mary Kay Executive Team who have so openly and candidly discussed the company to help with my research. Dick Bartlett in particular has guided me through this process. His leadership wisdom suffuses this book.

My appreciation goes to Richard Narramore for believing in this project and for his diligence in understanding the work. Every writer needs a supportive and insightful editor, and those words characterize Richard.

My literary agent, John Willig, has provided enthusiastic support through five books. His insight and candor throughout the process have been a great help.

I also want to express my appreciation to the many Mary Kay people who willingly spoke to me about their experiences at the company—no matter where I went or who I asked. This includes Gay on the executive floor, Jannette at the front desk, and numerous others I met on the elevator or lunch line. I am grateful for the contributions of Anne Newbury, Arlene Lenarz, and Doretha Dingler, each of whom gave me tremendous insight into the rich history of the company. I often find myself telling their success stories to my students at the university in the hope that they will discover their own potential. Their commitment to helping others is inspirational.

I have to thank the Heritage Department at Mary Kay Inc. Lisa Beegle was always there to help me find what I needed. Yvonne Pendleton must get credit for making this project work. She willingly gave of her time, provided reams of information, and made sure I got access to the people and stories that were critical to this book. She also made sure that I kept the facts straight. Thank you, Yvonne, for your help, guidance, and support in writing this book.

Jim Underwood
August 2002

Preface

For nearly three decades my answer to the question "How are you?" has never been anything but "*Great!*"

I must admit that as I close in on my seventieth birthday, feeling physically great is not always possible. But when I answer that question with "Great," I'm referring not to my physical state but to my emotional state.

Everyone at Mary Kay Inc. responds the same way to that question. Why? Because we all learned from Mary Kay Ash herself that there is no other acceptable answer. If you're ever in the vicinity of our world headquarters in Dallas, test us. Stop any employee and ask her how she is. I guarantee it, she'll be great.

Our leaders in particular take this lesson to heart. Occasionally people from outside our organization—and sometimes even new employees—challenge this response as insincere, even phony. But these cynics miss the essential point of what we take to be leadership. *Emotional leadership* is fundamental to leadership success. Leaders influence the emotional mindset of every individual within an organization.

Speaking for myself, I am mindful that *Great* cannot be insincere if it's going to work the way Mary Kay intended it to work. It must be values-driven, part of the ingrained culture of an organization. Thanks to Mary Kay, we have a purpose, and each of us believes he or she has a special duty to perform. We have elected to serve others and find great satisfaction in the giving.

Mary Kay called it our "Go-Give Spirit." Our purpose, or mission, is to *enrich women's lives.* Obviously, you can't do this unless your mindset is based on seeing the glass as half full. But as Jim Underwood explains in the following pages, we believe that you also can't fulfill the Mary Kay mission unless you follow the Golden Rule.

As to the "pink Cadillac" in this book's title, yes, that's the best-known image of our company—and probably one of the most recognizable symbols in the history of marketing. And yes, it's a form of recognition for an individual who has done an outstanding job of distributing our products, which happen to be cosmetics. But this "trophy on wheels" is a symbol of something far greater. It is a symbol of a whole way of doing business which we call the Mary Kay Way. This book provides insights into a unique and phenomenally successful business. It is a business that grew out of, and is still founded on, a simple set of powerful principles.

But let me start at the beginning.

Mary Kay Ash, our founder, had few advantages when she was young. But one that she did have was her mother's constant encouragement. "You can do it," the mother told the daughter, and the lesson stuck. It was sorely tested when Mary Kay started her career in direct sales as a Stanley Home Parties dealer just after World War II. She learned very quickly that she could not stand up at a Stanley party and explain to her hostess and guests that because she wasn't feeling well that evening, they would have to excuse her substandard demonstration. As Mary Kay liked to say, "That dog won't hunt." She knew she had to be . . . *great* or most likely there would be no sales and no profits, and her young family might go hungry.

After setting up her own company, she learned another lesson about the positive power of *Great!* When those around her became more positive because of her attitude, they became more enthusiastic, and performance soared. She often said, "Act enthusiastic and you'll be enthusiastic." She added, "Nothing great was ever accomplished without enthusiasm."

Mary Kay knew that in each human being there is a purpose; in her words, "God didn't have time to make a nobody—only a somebody." Many people outside our organization might consider these phrases trite, but they were one important way Mary Kay influenced other people's emotions and exerted her leadership. Management scholar John Kotter writes that leadership consists of creating a vision, aligning others to that vision, and then inspiring them to achieve the vision. In my opinion, no one in American business has done that better than Mary Kay Ash.

Mary Kay knew her purpose in life. She also knew somehow that her purpose was larger than her own life. When Morley Safer of TV's *60 Minutes* news magazine suggested that she was using God to further her own ambition, Mary Kay responded without hesitation that he had it backward: She sincerely believed that God was using *her* to accomplish *His* purposes.

She was confident that there was a grand pattern to her life. In the 30 years I knew her, I never saw her waver from her purpose, not once. I invite you to think how many people you've met about whom you'd say the same thing.

Mary Kay viewed her company as a *family*, a living community that she strove to perpetuate. She talked of P&L not as "profit and loss" but as "people and love." She knew that maximizing profits could not serve as the driving purpose of a company that hoped to sustain itself over decades. Make no mistake: Mary Kay knew profits were important, but they were only a means to an end. They would finance the next round of investments and make possible the next installment in a saga of enriching women's lives. She knew she had to be generous, investing in her employees and the members of her independent sales force. And she had to build binding ties of trust and loyalty, starting within the corporate "family" and extending all the way to her tens of millions of customers.

A few years ago, at the annual World Economic Forum (WEF) at Davos, Switzerland, I got into a public debate with Michael Hammer, who had just published his book *Reengineering the Corporation*, which was beginning to make waves in corporate America. I disagreed with Hammer on some key philosophical points having to do with reengineering, the central prescription of which seemed to boil down to the far less attractive process of downsizing. Since then, despite setbacks to the larger field of reengineering, downsizing is still rampant among U.S. corporations. Mass layoffs continued at a record high in the early years of the twenty-first century, with an average of almost 2 million workers expelled from their jobs annually.

Since that time downsizing seems to be corporate America's favored approach to increasing productivity and profits, enhancing shareholder value, and dominating global competition. Of the world's top 1,000 corporate leaders attending that WEF meeting, I'd guess a majority shared this view of corporate responsibility and leadership. In fact, in my 40 years of executive experience, which has included much contact with fellow business leaders, one version or another of this approach—vision and strategy couched in warlike, almost inhuman terms—has been the rule rather than the exception.

What's interesting—and troubling—about this is that employees in organizations view leadership in entirely different terms. They want their leaders to have high integrity, show respect, be honest, be fair, and even be compassionate.

Shouldn't we listen to them if we want their best?

I try to conduct myself as a "servant leader," and I suggest that the most effective leaders in history have had the same mindset. I really believe corporations can be major instruments of social change, as Mary Kay has been in empowering women. They also can serve a higher purpose, as in advancing women's health, funding cancer research, eliminating violence against women, and preserving the environment. I believe the success of future corporate leaders will be measured not by gargantuan profits, obscene executive stock options, and simple shareholder-wealth creation but by contributions to sustainable communities, ecosystems, and economies and—above all—as custodians of the human spirit. These elements should define and drive a leader's purpose.

Mary Kay got at her purpose in many ways both large and small. I distinctly recall our internal telephone directory when I joined the company in 1973. It was in alphabetical order by *first name*. She knew the value of operating like a small company, really more like an extended family. That practice still lives today. Top executives of this company (whose independent sales force numbers more than 900,000) still take the time to call each person who has a family tragedy—a health problem, an accident, or a death—to let each one know that we care, as an extended family, about her or him as an individual. We also remember birthdays and the Christmas holiday with a personal card, not to mention letters praising career accomplishments. It's vital to us to maintain the connectedness of a small, tightly knit family even though we have become a multi-billion-dollar enterprise.

When I was president of Mary Kay Inc. I insisted on taking every call that came to my office from the field sales organization. Thanks to our excellent customer service training, the vast majority of such calls that might have ended up in my office were answered satisfactorily before they reached me, but the offer stood. You probably can guess that as a hands-on leader, only steps down the hall from Mary Kay Ash, I *liked* being in touch with our customers. Truth be told, when our customer service improved to the extent that I started feeling out of things, I found a new way to stay personally connected. I would often slip down to the Director Information Services telephone bank, pop on a headset, and answer calls for a while. It wouldn't take me long to get a feel for the attitude of the field or to figure out where our next business challenge might be coming from.

I learned to listen carefully from Mary Kay. She believed that being a good listener is vital to being a good leader, and she made all of us around her believe that as well. But there was something more her leadership style required of me: to *think like a woman*. Mary Kay reminded me on more than one occasion that I was "thinking like a man" on some issue. That mindset simply won't cut it in a company with an independent sales force of nearly a million women, and so I and other males learned what, for lack of a better term, might be called "empathetic thinking." And we are better leaders for it.

Earlier, I noted that Mary Kay Ash had a sense of destiny. She also had a keen sense of her own mortality. In the early 1970s she personally took on the challenge—through books, speeches, videos, meetings, and other media—of making sure that her life's mission would carry on after her. She also knew she would need people who understood how to perpetuate her beliefs. As Jim Underwood explains, she focused on what she called "her" National Sales Directors, the top rank of the independent sales organization. She entrusted those leaders with her purpose, insisting over and over that they had to be prepared to carry on our mission when she no longer could.

The Nationals, as we affectionately call them, did take up her purpose when Mary Kay became ill and after her death on November 22, 2001. Few leaders have surrounded themselves with such an all-encompassing "succession plan," and few have executed it so masterfully.

Although she frequently operated in the realm of the visionary, Mary Kay also understood that we had to *implement* on a day-to-day level in order to perform our jobs excellently. When she hired her first employees, she developed a small pink card that spelled out our service promise to our customers in fine detail. Forty years later we still provide this card to new employees. Because of our relationships with our sales organization, and theirs with their customers, we have to be a "zero-tolerance" company in terms of implementation errors. Back orders are costly, of course, but we think of them in more human terms. They cause pain for both the salesperson and her customer. Shoddy or impolite service will cause the immediate and direct loss of a customer, but more than that, the customer will link any ill will to the person she bought the product from as well as the company whose name is on the package. We invest heavily in training and in state-of-the-art customer service contact programs, such as our Preferred Customer program and Internet programs, to ensure that our customers are surrounded by service.

Yet we realize that we can never do enough. Jim Underwood quotes one of our favorite Mary Kay sayings: "Never rest on your laurels. Nothing wilts faster than a laurel sat upon." As this book goes to press, the company is investing tens of millions more dollars in a new supply chain management system that will alter every employee's job within a year or two. When that program is complete, there will be another system improvement—and then another. When it comes to providing better customer service, change is constant.

The secret to coping with change in an environment like ours is to rely on what doesn't change: the values that drive our organization. Jim Underwood has appropriately made those values the centerpiece of his book, and we thank him for that. Mary Kay Inc. is composed of ethical leaders whose purpose does not waver. When we change, we do so because we think we have found a better way to accomplish our purpose. Our assumption is that if we change without reference to our purpose, we will get into trouble—and if we do that often enough, we will fail.

But we *won't* fail, because we've been taught by the master. We know our purpose. It's enriching women's lives.

Dick Bartlett, Vice Chairman
Mary Kay Inc.
August 2002

Introduction

A Different Kind of Company

I GET INTERESTING reactions when I tell people I've been studying the Mary Kay organization. "Oh," they say, "that's the company I've seen on the news . . . the one that gives out those pink Cadillacs." Almost everybody knows that much about Mary Kay Inc., but beyond a little knowledge of the company's products—cosmetics—few people outside the company know anything more.

Mary Kay Inc. is a lot more than a symbolic pink Cadillac. In fact, the reason why a business strategist like me was eager to write this book is that Mary Kay Inc. is one of the best-run and most successful companies in the world.

Consider the following:

- From its humble beginnings with a $5,000 investment by the founder, the company now does over $1.4 billion in global wholesale (which is $2.8 billion at retail) sales worldwide.
- Mary Kay Inc. is a leading e-business.
- The company has averaged double-digit growth almost every year of its existence.
- The company's global sales organization has operations in 33 countries.
- The company has 900,000 Independent Beauty Consultants worldwide.

I will explain how the company has achieved this extraordinary growth and success, but first I want to tell three short personal stories that relate to the larger story.

A Vendor Encounters Mary Kay Inc.

A number of years ago, as freshly minted masters of business administration (MBAs), a classmate and I decided we would go out into the world and put all the entrepreneurial knowledge we had recently gained to work. We had the opportunity to buy a small office products and furniture company, and we thought that would be a great place to get our start.

In those days my partner and I did it all. If a driver called in sick, we drove a truck. If a customer had a pressing need, one of us would jump in the car and deliver the customer's order. At night we stayed after hours and packed orders.

One of the first customers we acquired was a new company on the Dallas scene called Mary Kay Cosmetics. Although we were only a vendor of office products and furniture, it did not take us long to realize that not only was Mary Kay a growing company, it was an *unusual* company.

If you want to get an inside peek at a company, here's a really good strategy: Sell office furniture and then spend your days on the site putting the client's furniture together. It's amazing what you can see and hear when you put on a pair of blue jeans and a short-sleeved shirt and crawl around under desks, tightening bolts. You're invisible, and you will learn a lot.

My partner and I learned a lot about a lot of companies (some 400 in all) in those days. We heard the tirades of disgruntled executives and the demands for respect from subordinates. We saw it all. Most of it wasn't particularly surprising. It was more or less what we expected based on our prior life experiences and our business education.

But what we saw at Mary Kay Cosmetics was very different.

What we saw was enthusiasm, integrity, laughter, and excellence. At first we could not believe what we were seeing. Every employee was treated with the utmost respect. Even we, the vendors, were treated with respect. No matter what kind of day we had before going to Mary Kay, we knew we would leave there with lifted spirits.

As the company grew, we had the opportunity to get to know a lot of people who helped the founder, Mary Kay Ash, carry out her dream. When we encountered a problem, it was not unusual for someone in the sales group to drop what he or she was doing and help us solve it. Very often a staffer would want to share her enthusiasm for the company with us.

During the 10-year business relationship my partner and I had with Mary Kay, we often would talk about how different this organization was from other Fortune 500 companies that were our customers. At most of the other companies there was a certain kind of coldness. They did not seem to have enthusiasm for their jobs or their customers. A lot of the managers at the other companies had an aloof attitude toward subordinates. Certainly they didn't have much fun.

At Mary Kay it was just the opposite. They had fun and loved their customers, and it was clear that the managers loved to take a break and join in on the fun. By most qualitative measures, it was very, very different.

A Student Encounters Mary Kay Inc.

What is it that makes outstanding companies different? What is it that causes one company to be a marginal performer while another is flying straight for the heavens?

I discovered the answer to that question in 1991 while working on my doctorate in business administration. I was fortunate to study under Dr. H. Igor Ansoff, one of the world's leading experts in the field of strategy. What I discovered while studying under Dr. Ansoff was that companies that perform well meet a specific set of criteria. These principles that define high-performing organization have been the basis of my teaching and consulting ever since. I call them the "nine keys."

The difference between companies that meet these nine criteria and those that do not is striking. If a company meets them, it normally will produce profits between 100 and 300 percent higher than those of companies that do not.

I have had the chance to work with or study many excellent companies that observe most of the nine keys. Those companies include Southwest Airlines, Tricon (Pizza Hut, KFC, Taco Bell), and TMP Worldwide, to name a few. But in many of my consulting engagements, pride and resistance to change—especially from leaders at the large international companies—have stood in the way of making the necessary improvements. Most company leaders are simply unwilling to make the changes required to create an exceptional company.

When I started to study Mary Kay Inc. I was amazed to find that more than any other company I had encountered, it fit the criteria I was using to predict organizational success. Somehow, completely on her own, Mary Kay had discovered the strategic principles I had worked out in years of study with Dr. Ansoff and others. Far more important, of course, she had managed to build an organization that is based on those practices and principles.

The purpose of this book is to reveal these nine keys as they have been implemented at one exceptional company—Mary Kay Inc.—so that others may learn how to "fly straight for the heavens."

A Professor Encounters Mary Kay Inc.

When I made the move into academia as a professor in the field of management, one of the things I started doing at my university was to take graduate students out to major companies and do consulting. In a wonderful coincidence, one of my graduate students had the opportunity to complete a strategic analysis for Mary Kay Inc.

As the students finished their presentation to Richard (Dick) Bartlett, vice chairman and a longtime leader at the firm, he began talking to them about his perspective on the management practices and principles that had sustained the company. What I realized at that moment, belatedly, was that one of the best-managed companies in the world was in my own backyard. My experiences as a vendor and a student of management had pointed me in this direction, but it took my third exposure for me to finally get it.

I decided that the story of Mary Kay Inc.'s management practices had to be told. Eventually I asked Dick Bartlett for permission to do the research and write the book. The company routinely turns down movie and book opportunities, and so I wasn't optimistic about my prospects. I'm not sure whether my proposal included an appealing component missing from other such proposals or whether I was just persistent enough to wear down Dick Bartlett—not an easy task—but he and the company finally consented. The only guidance they offered was that they hoped my book would deliver on the promise in my proposal: to explain the leadership principles of their company.

In the course of researching this book I was invited to observe many meetings. One of the first was a "New Directors" conference at Mary Kay headquarters in Dallas. I must admit that in the back of my mind I was expecting to see a lot of stereotypical part-time beauty consultants who were full-time wives and mothers. What I found was a fascinating group of individuals from diverse backgrounds—almost a microcosm of American society. One woman sitting near me was a physical therapist. She had spent years to gain her educational and professional experience. It appeared that she was well positioned for a great career in a profession that is known for excellent compensation. Another was a dental hygienist. She had achieved the requirements for the sales director position in a few short months. She expected to surpass her hygienist salary with her Mary Kay income within three months. Another had owned her own business.

Others had a long history with the company, having been Independent Beauty Consultants for 10 or more years. Almost everyone had a unique story about how she had discovered Mary Kay and how the company had changed her life. For many the connection to the company started when they were customers. In almost every case they said they had been attracted to the independent sales force because of the attitudes, the camaraderie, and the enthusiasm they had seen in those who pursued a Mary Kay business.

While this zeal might be typical of a sales force, one would expect the management team at the corporation to have a different attitude. What I found at the company was the same level of enthusiasm I had found in the independent sales force. In numerous interviews with senior executives I observed that they also are personally touched by their experiences in this warm environment. Many say that what happened to them in their careers at Mary Kay is that they changed—in attitude, life goals, and, most important, their business philosophy.

Some might describe direct-sales companies as being a bit "cultlike" in nature. There is a strong culture in companies like Mary Kay, and while it may have originated with a single, charismatic individual—Mary Kay Ash herself—now the entire leadership team and the rank and file have taken up the cause. It is clear that after more than a decade and a half without Mary Kay Ash in day-to-day management, the firm is not at all dependent on her continued charismatic presence. It is, however, dependent on her principles.

Mary Kay Ash was held in the highest regard by everyone who had any contact with her, whether a person worked for the company or not. The firm's management endured some difficult times learning how to make the transition to her retirement and ultimately her passing. Interestingly, however, even as the firm went through those difficult times, sales continued to increase. In fact, except for a short period of time, the average annual sales increase has been in double digits.

What is it that has made this a successful company? Why do grown men become downright emotional and passionate when they relate Mary Kay Ash stories or, more important, when they talk about the countless lives she touched? Two things must be understood about the person, Mary Kay, and the company, Mary Kay Inc.

First, she lived the principles she taught. Her life's story of persevering and overcoming adversity illustrates what an individual can do if she sets her mind to it. Second, instead of focusing on herself (as a manager, a founder, and a person), she built a company on principles and practices that would lead to sustainable success. Regardless of whether she was leading the company, Mary Kay humbly built a giant of a company that, just like her, lived the principles and practices that she knew would sustain it. That was, after all, her dream in founding the company.

New Independent Sales Directors get to attend educational sessions in Dallas when they reach that first major milestone in their careers with the company. As part of the fun of that week, they get to participate in a tradition that dates all the way back to when Mary Kay Ash hosted the sessions in her home. When they come to the corporate headquarters, they are served cookies made from Mary Kay recipes. As a good-luck symbol they all have their pictures taken in Mary Kay's pink bathtub (a long-standing tradition), which is strategically placed in the president's office each month for these events. Before they leave, they also have the opportunity to have their picture taken holding a large replica of a pink Cadillac or to pose in front of headquarters with the real thing. These are not just photo ops; this is an opportunity to "make the commitment" to go for the pink Cadillac, and it paints an indelible picture of the success that is theirs for the working.

In order to earn a pink Cadillac an Independent Sales Director's unit must achieve wholesale production of $96,000 during a six-month qualification period. The pink Cadillac represents recognition of a unit's commitment to excellence and tenacity in achieving its goals. As many of the stories in this book will reveal, many of those who have achieved that goal had a long way to go and a lot of barriers to overcome to get there.

Interestingly, most Independent Sales Directors will tell you that the acquisition of the pink Cadillac is not that important to them. What is important is what it stands for. It means more than a pink Cadillac, much more. Women who have earned the pink Cadillac say that it represents one of the greatest personal achievements of their lives. It represents their own hard work and in many cases the determination it took to overcome significant obstacles in their lives during the process.

After reading this book or even this introduction, you may detect that I have a positive bias toward Mary Kay Inc. I can tell you that this company, as even its own executives mentioned in the interviews, is not perfect. It has flaws, and it makes mistakes just as any other company does. When I doggedly probed into sensitive areas of the company, without fail the executives I spoke with were honest and candid, and sometimes those discussions led to "off-the-record" sessions. However, I can assure you that nothing that is germane to the accuracy of the leadership story of this company has been left out.

Finally, it is important to realize that this is not a "company history." It is also not a book about the company's founder, Mary Kay Ash. It is not a book about the cosmetics industry or even about women or women in leadership positions. This is a book about principles of leadership that can be applied by anyone in any business setting. If you are a leader in an organization or aspire to be one, this is a book that can change your future. The principles revealed in the book already have influenced the lives of hundreds of thousands of men and women around the world. They can do the same for you and your organization. "If your mind can conceive it, and if you can believe it, you can achieve it." That was Mary Kay's way of saying that success is a choice. If you have the desire to be a successful leader, the principles revealed in this book will show you how.

SECTION I

THE FOUNDATION

1

How a Texas Entrepreneur Built a Global Company on the Philosophy of "Everyone Wins"

THE LEADERSHIP STORY of Mary Kay Inc. begins with the leadership story of the founder herself. It is a story of humble beginnings and great accomplishment.

It also is a story of winning against overwhelming odds.

Humble Beginnings

Mary Kathlyn Wagner was born on May 12, 1918, in Hot Wells, Texas, a tiny railroad and resort town that was headed toward extinction. For the Wagners, those were hard times and hard circumstances. The family soon relocated to Houston—then a rough southwestern city with fewer than 150,000 inhabitants—but the young girl's life scarcely improved. Beginning at the age of six, Mary Kay had to take care of her father, who suffered from tuberculosis, while her mother worked 14-hour days in a restaurant to support the family.

Even when things seemed to be going well for Mary Kay, hardship was never too far in the background. Many years later, for example, her young husband—the father of her three children—returned safely from World War II only to announce that he wanted a divorce. That left the young mother with three children to care for and dismal job prospects. In the working world of the 1940s, with GIs returning home and looking for work, there were not many career paths open to women.

One that *was* open to Mary Kay was direct selling, which appealed to her in part because it offered her the opportunity to work flexible hours and control her own financial destiny. She could sell quality products to women like herself, more or less on her own terms, while pursuing her dream of studying to become a doctor. She joined Stanley Home Products—a vendor of health- and home-care products since the early 1930s—and sold home-care products for it until 1952. After achieving phenomenal success as Stanley's top salesperson—success that ended all thoughts of a medical career—she was recruited by another direct-sales organization, World Gift, to serve as its Houston-area manager.

Within a few years she was promoted to national training director. In that position she was passed over for a promotion: The job was given to a man she had spent the previous year training. That pattern repeated itself several times. "[I kept] coming back to Dallas to find that one of those people was my superior," she recalled many years later. "If I could teach them how to do it, why couldn't I be the superior? But the real reason was, you are in the wrong body, honey!"[1] She left World Gift in 1963, when she realized that although she was working harder than her male counterparts and breaking sales records, she was earning much less than were those male colleagues.

Of course, the high-energy and ambitious Mary Kay, then in her mid-forties, wasn't about to retire. She decided to write a book detailing the things she had learned in her career and outlining her ideas for a better kind of direct-sales organization. After she had written up her "dream company," she realized that she had put a marketing plan on paper.

Not so coincidentally, there was a product she personally used that seemed perfect, something she *knew* she could sell. She once had done business with a cosmetologist—the daughter of an Arkansas hide tanner—who had introduced her to a skin-care product that Mary Kay thought was wonderful. She inquired about purchasing the skin-care secret, and eventually a deal was struck.

The Founding of a Dream

Thus, 1963 turned out to a big year for Mary Kay. She and her second husband decided to start a company to sell the skin-care product she had acquired. In founding the new company, Mary Kay set out to achieve two goals. First, she wanted to market a product of unquestionable quality and value, and she believed that the skin-care product to which she had acquired the rights met those standards. Second and more important, she wanted to offer women unlimited opportunity. "Those men didn't believe a woman had brain matter at all," she once said, reflecting on her former colleagues in direct sales. "I learned back then that as long as men didn't believe women could do anything, women were never going to have a chance."[2]

But creating opportunities for women was easier said than done. Mary Kay often recalled that when she started her company, a woman could not go to the bank and get a loan unless her husband cosigned the application. She knew from personal experience, moreover, that a woman was likely to be paid 50 cents for every dollar a man was paid for the same work. She understood how difficult it was for women trying to raise a family to work in traditional nine-to-five jobs. For all these reasons, Mary Kay wanted to be a part of changing the very fabric of the lives of working women.

She had $5,000 in personal savings that she was prepared to commit to this start-up company. The division of labor seemed promising: Her husband, an accomplished businessperson, understood the financials, and Mary Kay had the sales and marketing experience. But just a month before the company was to commence operations, Mary Kay experienced yet another tragedy. On August 13, 1963, her husband died at the breakfast table, the victim of a massive heart attack.

In her grief, she gathered her children around her to consider her future. She had already committed her $5,000 in savings, and she had just lost her partner. She considered giving up on the dream, but the combination of strong encouragement from her family and her own in-domitable spirit won out. Richard R. Rogers, her youngest son, quit his job in Houston to come help with the new company, taking over its operations. On September 13, 1963, the company officially went into business.

Later, her oldest son, Ben, joined them. Her daughter, Marylyn, was one of the first sales consultants. With Mary Kay and Richard at the helm and with the support of Ben, Marylyn, and others who believed in Mary Kay, Mary Kay Cosmetics was up and running.

The Foundation of Success: Principle-Based Leadership

Mary Kay was a devout Christian. She would discuss her beliefs freely, yet she often said that what you *did* was a lot more important than what you *said*. In developing the idea of her new company, she knew that if a company was to be really successful, it had to be founded on unchangeable principles and practices. That is, there had to be a set of principles, ideas that defined acceptable behaviors for a company that was determined to achieve excellence.

At the heart of Mary Kay's founding principles was her belief in the Golden Rule as a way to conduct business. Mary Kay believed that if she treated others—employees, vendors, and customers—as she herself wanted to be treated, her company would thrive. It was this simple yet powerful principle that drove everything Mary Kay did and everything she taught people to do.

At the beginning Mary Kay decided that the company would apply the Golden Rule to every business problem—even legal matters. This was unorthodox, to say the least. Most executives involved in corporate legal battles go on the offensive, taking an aggressive approach regardless of who is right or wrong. Not Mary Kay. And in those early days one new employee, an attorney, found out just how serious Mary Kay was in applying the Golden Rule to her business.

Brad Glendening—today the company's executive vice president, general counsel, and corporate secretary—wasn't just another attorney looking for a job. He was a trial lawyer and a very good one, at that. Trial lawyers, for those unfamiliar with the breed, are a species unto themselves. They could have coined the phrase "take no prisoners."

Glendening had seen numerous confrontations in court, where his cohorts in the legal profession didn't hesitate to launch an all-out assault on the victim. "Regardless of the circumstances, the trial lawyer's job is to discredit the opposition," explains Glendening. "It doesn't matter if it's a little old lady who was hit by a drunk driver; the typical trial lawyer is going to try to create doubt about the little old lady and her behavior in order to win the lawsuit."

Glendening came to Dallas in 1980 to interview for a position as a trial lawyer at one of the top law firms in the country. Along the way, however, he also got an overture from another Dallas company: Mary Kay Cosmetics. One thing led to another, and the trial lawyer ultimately became convinced that the job at Mary Kay was the one he should take. When an offer came, he accepted, and his first assignment after being hired was to go to meet the firm's founder, Mary Kay Ash.

"I look back on that day and shudder to think about what might have happened to my chances at that meeting," recalls Glendening. "Here I walk into this meeting with my brazen attitude, a giant frizzy haircut, and my nonconformist Earth Shoes on. I must have looked more like a sideshow barker than a professional, but that's the way trial lawyers dressed and behaved. I really did not look like someone who would fit into a first-class organization."

The meeting with Mary Kay went well, Glendening recalls. His new employer did not seem to pay much attention to his appearance, evidently focusing instead on who he was as a person. She was gracious and seemed honestly interested in him as an individual. Toward the end of the meeting she looked over at Virgil Pulliam, the corporate attorney who had hired Brad, and asked Pulliam if he had explained the firm's legal policy to the new hire. Pulliam affirmed that he had, but Mary Kay apparently decided to make sure that Glendening understood how the firm ran its legal affairs. She looked Glendening in the eye and said, "We do what's right. Try to never forget that."

That statement would have a significant impact on the rest of Brad Glendening's life. At first he did not understand the implications of what Mary Kay had said. Once he really grasped what she meant, it took him a while to believe that a company could succeed in business doing that. What she meant, simply stated, was that the company would not engage in some of the practices that had permeated the legal profession. Rather than attacking and destroying the credibility of a victim, for example, the corporate policy at Mary Kay was to make sure that the firm accepted responsibility for a wrong and worked to correct the situation.

"It was a total reversal for me and contradicted everything I'd been taught in law school," Glendening explains. "What I discovered was that this was not only policy, it was expected behavior. You didn't approach people as adversaries if you had made a mistake. If we did make a mistake, we went the extra mile to make sure that our error resulted in the fair and equitable treatment of the wronged party. It was not an issue of creating a legal defense; it was an issue of making sure we did the right thing."

When Everyone Wins

Almost every person who worked directly with Mary Kay has a story like Brad Glendening's to tell about her uncanny ability to define the moment, to stand up for what she believed, and to promote the Golden Rule.

It is nearly impossible to spend any time at Mary Kay Inc. without hearing a reference to one or more of her sayings. When confronted with a business challenge, many managers summon up a relevant Mary Kay quote to persuade themselves or their colleagues that a certain course of action is the right one. They do this without embarrassment and without any hint that they're doing what's called for. They appear to believe genuinely that Mary Kay's wisdom is as relevant today as it was decades ago.

This leads to two observations. First, Mary Kay clearly had something powerful to say. (Reading one of her books will reveal just how "leading-edge" this woman was as a management thinker.) Second and perhaps even more important, she gave her wisdom tenacious roots by making sure that the people around her understood and embodied that wisdom. Some leaders "manage" their companies; others provide a foundation of leadership that inspires the people around them—and the people who will follow them—to achieve success.

Mary Kay was in the latter category. As the company grew, she realized that she could not manage every aspect of a global operation. She realized too that only principled leadership at every level of the organization could propel the company toward the kind of success she had only dreamed of back in the early days, when she had first thought about turning her ideas into a living, breathing company. She took steps to ensure that everyone associated with the company understood and embraced the principles that stood behind the organization—and thereby created a "principled organization."

Dick Bartlett was another individual who learned early on that Mary Kay "lived her ethics" and that her company did as well. Over a 30-year period Bartlett has held key positions with the company, including executive vice president of marketing, president, and vice chairman. In a recent interview he reflected on the importance to the company of a consistent ethical position in the context of an industry that has not always been known for that stance:

> *There is no doubt that good ethical practices are good for business. As president of Mary Kay and chairman of our industry association, I led the effort to update its code of ethics based on Mary Kay's long-established code. Our policies guaranteed the repurchase of inventory [purchased within the last year] from sales consultants who wished—for any reason—to leave the business. Mary Kay also has a 100 percent, no questions asked, customer satisfaction guarantee.*
>
> *The new Direct Selling Association (DSA) code that we helped develop and get adopted in the United States has been ratified by the World Federation of Direct Selling Associations and thus covers some 1,000 companies represented by 40 million independent salespeople in more than 100 countries.*
>
> *Why is this good for business? Well, this code hasn't only served to protect consumers of our products, services, and opportunities but has also enhanced our government relations with state attorneys general, the U.S. Federal Trade Commission, and equivalent institutions throughout the world. Our industry is now sought out to help developing nations establish workable consumer protection programs. And last but not least, our self-regulatory code enforcement actions have gained us the respect of consumer advocates as well.*

Thus, a strong ethical stance not only makes a company stronger internally but also helps it within its industry and in its relations with regulators, legislators, and consumers. Mary Kay didn't necessarily anticipate all these benefits when she founded her business on ethical grounds, but she certainly was pleased that they accrued to her company.

Growing to Greatness

In 1964 the company held its first "Seminar." This is the company's term for the convention that is held each year in Dallas at which the top performers of the year are recognized. Five successive back-to-back groups of Mary Kay independent sales force members fill the Dallas Convention Center for more than four weeks. Yes, it's a business meeting, but the pageantry and trappings that accompany it sometimes call to mind a coronation. There are diamonds, lots of diamonds. And of course there are pink Cadillacs, bestowed upon those who have kept their commitment to "be great." Inspiration and motivation are the overarching themes, sounded constantly throughout the convention.

By the time the first Seminar kicked off in 1964, the company had leveraged Mary Kay's original investment of $5,000 into nearly $198,000 in wholesale sales. This was a remarkable feat at that time. Things definitely were looking up for the company and for Mary Kay as well. In 1966 she married Mel Ash. Mel was her husband and her mainstay and chief cheerleader until his death in 1980.

The company went public in 1968, and by 1976 it had grown to the point where it met the requirements for being listed on the New York Stock Exchange (NYSE). Richard R. Rogers was president of the company at that time and thus become one of the youngest men ever to head an NYSE-listed company.

But being a public company, especially one listed on the NYSE, meant that the corporation was making decisions to satisfy shareholders as well as being under pressure to produce strong numbers on a quarterly basis. Mary Kay disapprovingly referred to this financial phenomenon as "quarteritis" and became increasingly uncomfortable with it as a driving force for her company's direction.

Another factor began to come into play. There were those in the direct-marketing industry whose practices did not meet the standards practiced by Mary Kay Inc. As others watched her success in direct marketing, some saw an opportunity to "get rich quick" by using pyramid schemes and other approaches that were clearly not in the best interest of those who became involved. In a number of cases people were left with a garage full of "inventory" and no one to sell to. From the beginning Mary Kay made it clear that her company would have no part of any such practice. "If people seek the best for others," she was fond of saying, "the profits will follow."

By 1983 Mary Kay's $5,000 initial investment, plus the subsequent public offering and reinvested capital, provided the foundation for more than $300 million in sales annually. But for the reasons outlined above, the company's senior management was less and less happy about being a publicly traded company. Of course, they were not alone in reaching this conclusion; many companies that had gone public in the late 1970s and early 1980s were reversing course, setting in motion plans to buy back their stock from the public and once again become privately held.

In 1985, therefore, Mary Kay and other investors borrowed the funds necessary to take the company private again, a transaction that went smoothly and has proved to be a good strategy for both the company and its investors. As a privately held company, Mary Kay Inc. has continued to grow at phenomenal rates. It is difficult for any company to grow by double-digit percentages over long periods of time—as the base gets bigger, growth is harder to sustain on a percentage basis—but this company has managed to do that almost every year.

In 1987, after 24 years at the helm, Mary Kay decided it was time to step down. She assumed the title of chairman emeritus—although agreeing to remain active as a motivational leader—and Richard R. Rogers became chairman of the board.

How the Independent Sales Force Is Structured

Since I'll be referring to Mary Kay Inc.'s "independent sales force" throughout this book, it will be helpful for the reader to have a sense of how it is structured.

Mary Kay Inc. provides a clearly defined career path for its independent sales force members. Every one of them begins her business in the same way: by signing an Independent Beauty Consultant agreement and purchasing a starter kit. The consultants sell cosmetics and skin-care products and earn a commission on those sales. A key point is that each consultant is in business for herself. Consultants are in a contractual relationship with the company throughout their Mary Kay careers.

The earnings opportunities available to these independent contractors increase as they climb the Mary Kay "ladder of success," all the way up to the highest position within the independent sales force, that of an Independent National Sales Director.

Here are the positions, rung by rung:

Independent Beauty Consultant

All consultants, no matter where they are on the career path, are eligible for product discounts from the company as well as quarterly rewards and prizes.

- As personal team members are added, there is the opportunity to earn personal team commissions and bonuses.
- An Independent Beauty Consultant also has the opportunity to earn the use of a Mary Kay career car.

Independent Sales Director

Once she has proved her expertise in selling Mary Kay products and sharing the career opportunity, a consultant enters a qualification period during which time she must demonstrate her abilities in these areas to reach another step on the career path, that of Independent Sales Director. She can earn

- Personal team commissions
- Unit volume commissions and bonuses
- Unit development bonuses
- A luxury Top Sales Director trip
- The use of a Pontiac Grand Prix or a Cadillac

Additional earnings opportunities are available as an Independent Sales Director develops offspring Sales Directors and progresses to the higher career path positions of Senior Sales Director, Future Executive Senior Sales Director, Executive Senior Sales Director, and Elite Executive Senior Sales Director.

Independent National Sales Director

When an Independent Sales Director has developed a predetermined number of first-line and second-line offspring Sales Directors, she can reach the position that is the pinnacle of the Mary Kay career path, Independent National Sales Director (NSD). In this position she is eligible to earn

- Personal team commissions
- Personal unit volume commissions
- First-line offspring commissions
- Second-line and third-line offspring commissions
- New first-line offspring Sales Director debut bonuses
- Offspring National Sales Director debut bonuses ($10,000 annually)
- A luxury NSD trip
- The use of a Cadillac
- Other miscellaneous incentives

Independent National Sales Director Emeritus

At the end of her distinguished career, an Independent National Sales Director debuts as a National Sales Director Emeritus, at which time she is eligible

- For the Family Security Program
- To keep the National Sales Director pink Cadillac she has been driving
- In the first five years, to take three of the luxury National Sales Director trips of her choice
- For recognition when she attends company events

Today there are more than 900,000 individuals in 33 countries around the world who are active members of the company's independent sales force.

A Broader Mission

Over the years, the founding purpose of the firm evolved into what is currently a part of the company's formal mission statement: *to enrich women's lives.*

As the years went by this purpose gained scope and momentum. Early in the history of the company Mary Kay realized that her largely female independent sales force represented a microcosm of the larger world—both good and bad. It disturbed her greatly, for example, when she read statistics on cancer rates among women, and she had seen personally the pain and trauma experienced by employees and Independent Beauty Consultants who had been afflicted with cancer. In response, she urgently wanted to do something to help find a cure for cancer.

In 1996 the Mary Kay Ash Charitable Foundation was established. The initial mission of the foundation was to focus on research on cancers that affect women. At the turn of the century, sensing another problem that was in itself a "cancer" on our society, the foundation added to its agenda the prevention of domestic violence against women. Mary Kay's estate has contributed generously to the foundation and its efforts to fight cancer and domestic violence.

More Than Just a Rich History

As with almost everything else about Mary Kay Inc., there is much more to tell than can be contained in a few short chapters. Perhaps a personal recollection can stand in for some of those missing details.

In the early 1970s this writer owned a company that did business with Mary Kay Inc. To an outsider, particularly one involved in trying to make a small business succeed, one of the most impressive things about Mary Kay Inc. was how *proud* everyone who worked at Mary Kay was of the company. One employee, demonstrating a strong "pride of owner-ship," insisted on conducting a tour of a manufacturing plant.

A second impressive thing was the level of sophistication on display in that factory. The plant, designed with energy efficiency in mind, was a state-of-the-art facility that has since received numerous awards for its innovative approaches to manufacturing. For example, all the incoming raw materials were delivered to an elevated area in the plant. Those mate-rials were put into bins with pipes leading to various manufacturing sta-tions. Pulled by gravity alone, the raw materials were delivered to the production line, where they were used to make Mary Kay products, pack-aged, and prepared for shipping.

Another innovative development has been the merging of the com-pany's operations with the Internet. Today Mary Kay Inc. is an industry leader in its e-commerce revenues, an astounding feat in itself and one that also permits greater supply chain efficiencies, increased revenue, and higher profitability. It is the ultimate marriage of high tech and high touch.

These examples suggest that despite Mary Kay's gradual disengage-ment from day-to-day business, the company will continue to break new ground. Her daily involvement in the firm ceased when she suffered a major stroke in 1996. In June 2001, during an unusual period of stress for the company, Richard R. Rogers returned to take the helm. Mary Kay passed away later that year, on November 22.

As her colleagues celebrated her life and mourned her death, the giant Mary Kay independent sales force rallied to make March 2002 a record-breaking month. Meanwhile, recruiting—a key challenge in direct sales—was rebounding. These twin successes suggest again that the company's heritage, practices, and momentum will provide a solid foundation for the future.

The Greatest

For all her accomplishments Mary Kay was never really recognized for what she was. One reason is that as competitive as she was, she never liked to get into comparisons of herself with others. But the facts speak for themselves.

Along with her family members and colleagues, she parlayed a $5,000 investment into a $2 billion-plus company with 900,000 independent beauty consultants in 33 countries.

She established the practices and principles that made that enormous achievement possible. She had *vision* and was able to persuade others to share in that vision.

When people talk about the company today, they are most likely to talk about pink Cadillacs without knowing what those symbols mean to legions of accomplished and ambitious women. They don't understand the leadership example that stands behind those symbols.

As Mary Kay often said, "This is about so much more than lipstick." It's about more than pink Cadillacs. This is the story behind the story, an analysis of a cosmetics company that teaches some of the best lessons on American enterprise, entrepreneurship, values, and ethics. It is the story of one of the best-run companies that American industry has ever seen.

Notes

1. From Mary Kay Ash's acceptance speech after she was honored by Northwood University as its 1990 Outstanding Business Leader (www.northwood.edu/obl/1990/ash.html).
2. Quoted in a *Texas Monthly* article from 1995 (http://slick.org/deathwatch/mailarchive/mag00394.html).

2

Character Counts: Lessons
from the Master Herself

MANY CORPORATE EXECUTIVES focus principally on results. Exceptional leaders focus on the behaviors that *create* results.

At first glance this difference may not appear to be significant. In fact, it is substantial. Anyone who has run an organization realizes that it is possible to use threats and high-pressure tactics to achieve a short-term goal. In some cases, though, managers try to use those tactics on a long-term basis. It doesn't work. Those managers may win some short-term battles, but in the long run they will lose the war. In most cases good people leave companies run by those people, and in the end such a company will lack both talent and continuity.

Thus, in the end it comes down to one simple issue: How are people treated?

Great leaders treat people well. They inspire people to achieve more than they ever dreamed they could. Great leaders build up instead of tearing down.

Mary Kay Ash understood and lived the idea of achieving performance by building up the behaviors that produce performance. She realized that long-term success is founded on people and on seeking the very best for them.

Before she talked about how people should be led, Mary Kay Ash demonstrated her leadership principles by example—in the way she led others. She went to great lengths to ensure that those around her saw firsthand that each leadership lesson she taught was practical and would work. That is why any book about the leadership of the company has to talk about the leadership of its exceptional founder.

Mary Kay the Manager

There are executives who come into an organization, seize the reins, and push that organization in new directions. They shake things up and force people out of their ruts, and in some cases the company begins to perform. In most of these cases, though, when those executives leave the company, it reverts to its former state and its old problems return. Why? Because the organization was dependent on the leader for direction and motivation.

There are a few leaders who are able to create a different type of organization. Those leaders lead by practice and principle. That is, rather than "strong-arming" an organization into achieving performance, they seek to instill certain practices and principles that will enable the organization to achieve and sustain high levels of performance even after they are gone.

Mary Kay Ash was that kind of executive. She realized that only by developing a set of practices and principles could she affect the way the firm did business around the world.

As was noted in Chapter 1, Mary Kay founded her business on what she called Golden Rule management. Again, the Golden Rule simply states that you should treat others the way you want to be treated. ("Do unto others," as Jesus put it, "as you would have them do unto you.") It's interesting that although almost all religious traditions include some version of the Golden Rule, it is not commonly a part of business, at least as practiced by contemporary business leaders.

Mary Kay was different. She realized early on that she needed to establish this simple principle as a practice in her organization or she would never be able to achieve the lofty goals she had for Mary Kay Cosmetics. The power of that insight becomes obvious when one looks at her book *Mary Kay on People Management.* The first chapter of the book is all about the principle and the practice related to the Golden Rule, and every subsequent chapter harks back to that rule as the company's founding premise.

Why don't more individuals and companies live by the Golden Rule? For one thing, it's not easy. In the case of people, it requires a distinct set of attributes and attitudes.

The Six Virtues of a Great Leader

The six virtues of a great leader are: humility, a desire to seek the best for others, high expectations of excellence from those around them, integrity, impatience with the status quo, and a certain indomitable spirit or energy.

What did Mary Kay start with? When she founded her company, she had $5,000—a small fortune to her but a relatively small sum by most business measures—her knowledge of direct selling, a great product, and her character.

Which of these factors was most important to the subsequent success of the company? Without a doubt it was character. "What you are speaks so loudly." Mary Kay was fond of saying, "I can't hear what you say." The stronger the character of the leader is, the more likely it is that the leader will be successful in guiding a company.

The people at Mary Kay Inc. loved and respected Mary Kay Ash because of how she treated them. They loved her because of her expectations of excellence and the way she got them to achieve things they did not believe were possible. They loved her because she was there for them in times of tragedy. Her timeless beliefs and strong principles set the example that the company's management and the independent sales organization still seek to emulate.

In order to understand how Mary Kay Ash inspired this kind of loyalty—to understand how she exerted her character—it is necessary to understand more about the standards by which she lived her life. I will refer to these standards as "virtues," but you may choose to substitute another word. The point is not the label but the ideal behind the label.

Humility

All people long to be valued and recognized for their contributions to something outside themselves. This search for what might be called significance is the most powerful and important force in relationships.

People tend to build their significance in one of two ways: by taking it from others or by recognizing the significance of others. Most of us engage in the former; that is, we build our significance at the expense of others. But a smaller group of people, whom I refer to as humble people, invest significance in those around them. They treat others as their equals—regardless of their position in life at that particular point in time—and value their contributions. In other words, they are honestly humble.

Brad Glendening recalls how Mary Kay used to behave at important public events, for example, those attended by other chief executive officers (CEOs) and executives, celebrities, and so on. Many of her counterparts would make a grand entrance at such events, but Mary Kay tended to enter the room quietly. Where others were inclined to grandstand and seek the limelight, Mary Kay was more likely to make her way to an out-of-the-way corner of the room, where she would chat with the people who happened to be there. Not that she was shy or antisocial—in fact, far from it. But she signaled through her behavior that she cared little about personal recognition and was far more concerned about those around her. "She was this way around everybody," Glendening explains. "Always making *you* feel important."

Those who seek to build their own significance at the expense of others create organizations that are monuments dedicated to themselves. Humble leaders like Mary Kay build organizations that are dedicated to those they serve, that is, their customers and their employees.

Hundreds of stories are told by members of her independent sales force as well as by employees at corporate headquarters about how Mary Kay called personally to check on them and boost their spirits in a time of personal challenge. And it wasn't only in times of crisis that this priority manifested itself. On one occasion, for example, Mary Kay was in Washington on business. She was scheduled to leave in the evening to return to Dallas to attend a meeting with a group of new employees at the firm. During her stay in Washington she got a call inviting her to attend a reception with the President in the White House; for most people this would be a once-in-a-lifetime opportunity. She thanked the White House staffers for the invitation but declined. Why? Because she honestly believed that her commitment to the new hires was far more important than socializing with the President of the United States.

Seeking the Best for Others

Another virtue characteristic of Mary Kay was her desire to seek the best for others. We all have run across managers who prevent their good people from getting a promotion either because losing them might mean lower unit performance or because a manager is afraid of competition. I have run across people who actually have sabotaged a colleague's reputation so that others in the firm would not want to hire him or her. And this "looking out for number one" attitude has gained great currency in the popular management literature in recent years. Think, for example, of books like *Why SOBs Win and Other Lose* and *The Management Secrets of Attila the Hun.*

Great leaders are not SOBs or Attila the Hun. In fact, they are exactly the opposite. Great leaders seek the best for others.

A skeptic might ask: "If a company's overriding objective is to maximize profits, doesn't that sometimes entail running over individuals who get in the way of that objective, whether inside or outside the firm?"

Mary Kay didn't think so. She believed that the only way to maximize profits was to maximize people. Unless you are focused on seeking the best for others, beginning with your own people, you cannot be successful. In the early years of the company Mary Kay fought a lot of battles with investment bankers and others over this issue. They argued for an increased emphasis on the bottom line; she argued for investing in people. And on this score she never gave in.

One might also question whether the twenty-first-century distillation of the company's founding principle—"to enrich women's lives"— fits with seeking the best for others. Are men included under the umbrella of this mission statement?

The short answer is yes. Although Mary Kay focused her efforts on women, she applied the concept to everyone in the organization. The Mary Kay corporate organization has always included a large number of talented men. Why? Because Mary Kay made it a point to find and retain the brightest people regardless of their gender. She applied the "seek the best for others" principle to everyone in her organization. This is a virtuous circle: Having the best people around is one of the best ways to *keep* the best people around.

One test of this principle is to examine how people are treated when they voice the intention to leave the organization. In Mary Kay's case, she never took offense when associates confessed that they were tempted to move on to what were apparently greener pastures. She never discouraged someone from pursuing a dream and in fact enjoyed talking with people about their dreams. Why? Because she truly wanted the best for others. At the same time, if Mary Kay became convinced that someone's decision to leave the company meant that he or she was *giving up on a dream*, she didn't hesitate to wade in and attempt to influence that individual's way of thinking.

From time to time, of course, people did leave the company for greener pastures. Notably, a significant percentage of these individuals eventually came back, in part because the new opportunity turned out to be not as good as expected and in part because of their recollection of how they had been treated at Mary Kay. Of course Mary Kay would welcome them back not only because they were talented people who could help the company but also because she believed that coming back into the fold would be good for them. Not many companies are that welcoming when the prodigal son returns home!

The same rules apply to the Mary Kay independent sales force. Although, as was noted in Chapter 1, the members of this group operate as independent contractors, more than a few of these women have told stories about leaving the fold and then being welcomed back. For example, in response to a family crisis, a salesperson might decide that she had to cut back on—or even give up entirely—her Mary Kay business. In such situations the way Mary Kay Ash reacted—and the way her company responded—spoke volumes. "Go attend to your family's needs now," the word would come down. "This business will be there for you when you decide to return." For a self-employed woman facing difficult circumstances this kind of reassurance could make an enormous difference.

Similarly, in times when the primary breadwinner for a family might be laid off or left without a paycheck, Mary Kay Ash was always quick to bolster a woman's confidence that she could replace that income with newfound attention to her Mary Kay business. "Treat this as you would any full-time career, and the rewards will come," she would say.

Expecting Excellence

Some managers achieve results by nitpicking and verbally abusing their subordinates. Other leaders set extraordinarily high standards of excellence for those around them—and, even more important, set outrageously high goals for themselves—and then motivate and inspire others to achieve those goals.

When she started Mary Kay Cosmetics, Mary Kay had some outrageous goals. She wanted to offer a quality product surpassing that of competitors. She wanted to make a difference in the lives of women at a time when women had little opportunity. She also wanted to prove a few things about herself, about women, and about people in general. Mary Kay held a deep belief that if you created a company that is based on exceptionally high standards of excellence and made it clear that you believed that *everyone could achieve far beyond his or her own estimates of his or her ability,* people would respond. And they did.

Exceptionally high standards of excellence means that you have high expectations for yourself first and for others second. Mary Kay always taught her independent sales force leaders that they should never expect anyone to do something they had not already done. She would look at people, and instead of seeing an underperformer, she would see a Mary Kay person who hadn't yet lived up to her potential. She led not by disciplining but by instilling in others the discipline needed to achieve the lofty heights of their potential.

In Texas we have a saying: "It's not about the dog in the fight . . . it's all about the fight in the dog." Success and achievement are more about attitude than they are about innate talent. Great managers understand that by expecting outrageous excellence, they are encouraging people to achieve their potential. They are asking others to make a commitment to maximizing who they are. The result in many cases is a new level of excitement and enthusiasm.

What greater gift can you give someone than to help that person understand just how capable and gifted he or she is? This is the gift that hundreds of thousands of women say Mary Kay Ash gave them.

Tom Whatley, president of global sales and marketing, explains this phenomenon succinctly. "The Mary Kay story," he says, "is about people who choose to achieve great things in spite of their circumstances."

Like Mary Kay herself, the company expects outrageous excellence. Regardless of background, experience, training, or aptitude, every person is expected to realize his or her potential fully. But only a great leader can persuade others to strive for such exceptional goals.

Integrity

J. R. Ewing, the guy-you-love-to-hate character from the prime-time soap opera *Dallas*, once made an interesting statement: "Contracts are written to be broken, but a man's word is a bond that must be kept."

He was referring to a time-honored tradition in the "oil patch" of Texas. Many of those who worked in the Texas oil industry came from families and businesses that placed a high value on integrity. In the oil patch, when the timely delivery of a piece of equipment might mean the difference between dramatic success and heartbreaking failure, business-people often did not have time to draw up a contract. They had to be able to trust one another. Over the years the tradition developed in the oil patch that if you gave your word, you *kept* it—no questions, no excuses, no nothing. You kept your word or you broke your pickax trying.

That's the kind of integrity Mary Kay Ash had. As an associate once said of her, "Mary Kay told the truth, regardless of the cost. And in some cases it cost her." But there is more to the story. Because of the integrity she so clearly embodied, people wanted to do business with her and work for her. Many at the company who have worked elsewhere talk of the "different world" out there. Mary Kay employees take comfort and satisfaction in the integrity of their organization, and in the long run this drives performance.

Impatience with the Status Quo

The business world is nothing like it was 15 or 20 years ago. A company can't sit on its historical success factors and hope that tomorrow will look like yesterday. Rapid change and unpredictability are here to stay. Successful companies must be prepared for nearly continuous change.

This is certainly true in the cosmetics industry. Mary Kay Inc. and the firm's competitors have been hit with successive jolts over the last decade or so. Changes in societal patterns, customer preferences, and buying habits, among many others, have turned the cosmetics world upside down not once but many times. Mary Kay Inc. has responded with constant innovation and risk taking in a concerted effort to keep the company from becoming complacent.

Mary Kay often said she wanted to find people who would take risks for the company. She wanted people in her sales force who would dare to do extraordinary things with their lives. Not surprisingly, she expected no less from the people in the company's research and development department. The result has been a steady stream of new products that have kept up with and sometimes even defined the latest trends in the industry. This is challenging the status quo and creating the *next* status quo that will need to be challenged.

An Indomitable Spirit

There is a subtle thread running through the dramatic success stories of the top performers in the independent sales force today and throughout the history of Mary Kay Inc. By any logical accounting, most of them should not have been so successful. Many had long odds working against them. Many had to surmount enormous obstacles to become top performers. But as Mary Kay was fond of pointing out, Thomas Edison failed many times before succeeding at his inventions. (He tried literally thousands of materials before stumbling on the right material to serve as a filament in a lightbulb.) The same can be said of almost everyone who becomes a great leader. Fortune recently published a list of individuals who were high achievers by almost any measure. The list included people like Albert Einstein and General Douglas MacArthur. At the end of the list of names there was a note about the disability each person on the list had to overcome to achieve success in his or her career.

Very few of us are born with everything we need to be successful. The logical conclusion therefore is that success has less to do with our ability and much more to do with our commitment to achieve excellence in spite of our shortcomings.

Letters to Mary Kay Inc.

It strikes me that adding some additional voices to this discussion might be helpful. As you might expect, Mary Kay Inc. receives an unending stream of letters from people whose lives have been touched by the company in one way or another. They may be employees, Independent Sales Associates, or friends and family members of people associated with the company. Collectively, these letters give a glimpse into what can happen at companies that make a commitment to live by the six virtues. Here are examples:

> *Fifteen years ago my mom was a single mother living paycheck to paycheck. . . . This company has given us so much. I appreciate what she has done for me and how much fun it was seeing how much she has grown as a person from the beliefs of this company. There is no money that would replace that. I now have a Mary Kay business, as does my sister. It's amazing how much fun we have.*
>
> —*Jackie Wagener*

Sharon Stempson is a Mary Kay Independent National Sales Director whose daughter wrote her this letter, which she then forwarded to the company:

> *I can't tell you how many times I have called on lessons from my childhood in a Mary Kay home in my own life and career. I never understood how foreign goal setting, self-awareness, self-*

confidence, and a positive attitude were to most of the popula-
tion until I ventured out into the real world. Now that I am a
mother, I realize just how fortunate I am to have you as my con-
fidante, motivator, and mentor. I felt the need to tell you these
things because I find myself giving some serious thought as to
how I might positively influence [my son] Michael's life and val-
ues in the years to come. My prayer every night while I am giv-
ing Michael his bottle before bed is that I can be the parent you
have been to me, Mom. That I may raise my son to value God,
himself, his family, and those around him. That I may instill in
Michael the confidence you have instilled in me to be whatever
I dream to be. That Michael may see me touching other people's
lives profoundly the way you have touched so many lives. I get
nervous when I realize what big shoes I have to fill, but then I
remember I was raised to believe that "whatever you can dream
and believe, you can achieve."

I remember staring out of my seventeenth-floor office window at
the people in the skyscraper across the street and wondering if
they were as unfulfilled and unchallenged as I was in my man-
agement position at a major corporate securities firm. Today,
three short years later, I am a wonderfully fulfilled Independent
Sales Director. I love driving my pink Cadillac with two child
seats in the back. I have the opportunity to stay home with my
children while having a professional outlet. Mary Kay has
really been the missing puzzle piece to a complete life.
                                                    —Lisa Allison

After she buried her three-day-old infant, Autumn Kelley began
receiving cards and letters from Mary Kay corporate offices as well as
from members of the sales force. In response she wrote:

It really was overwhelming. I began to realize what a truly won-
derful company this is. Think about it. How many Beauty Con-
sultants are there? But I was important enough for these people
to take time out of their busy day to send me a card or letter of

encouragement. . . . I have worked in many places and have never seen anything like it. I would like to thank Mary Kay Ash for starting such a wonderful company and tell the people who carry on her dream that I know she is beaming with pride. If you are out there wondering if you can really do this or questioning if this is really for you, if you want to be involved in a business where people are concerned about you, want nothing more than for you to achieve your dreams, then you're right where you belong.

Debbie Kimzey was a college student on a full athletic scholarship and on the women's NCAA equestrian team when she used her last $100 to purchase a starter kit for a Mary Kay business. She did that so that she could let go of one of her three jobs. She did very well before battling an illness that sent her spirits and her paychecks plummeting to a low of negative $22. With her mother's encouragement, Debbie staged a comeback over the last two years that earned her the use of a pink Cadillac, unit recognition, and a healthy income. She wrote:

In any other business I would've lost my position and possibly would have never gotten it back. "Thank you, Mary Kay, for always believing in us. Belief is the only thing that helped me through being sick. Mary Kay allows us to believe big and achieve whatever we are willing to work for.

Walking the Talk

In the course of researching this chapter I spoke on the phone with someone who had worked with Mary Kay for many years. I read her my list of six "virtues"—humility, seeking the best for others, expecting excellence, integrity, impatience with the status quo, and an indomitable spirit—and read a brief description of each one. She listened carefully as I went through the list. Then I asked if they added up to an accurate description of how Mary Kay led the firm. When she responded, you could almost hear the smile in her voice. "That's exactly how she lived her life," the woman said.

What's interesting about that story is not that I "got it right." (Given the consistency of the stories I was hearing, getting it right was not all that difficult.) What's interesting was that my interviewee didn't hesitate to agree with my characterization: *That's exactly how she lived her life.* Clearly, there was and is a shared vision out there of what Mary Kay's life was all about.

But again, my main point is that the way Mary Kay lived her life served as a template for the way the company lives its life. You succeed by helping others succeed. Their success is your success, and if they don't succeed, it's unlikely that you will either.

Here is an example: The Mary Kay independent sales organization operates without any assigned territories. That means a woman can add members to her sales team from any part of the country. She can be sure that one of her colleagues will serve as a local contact for this person. Interestingly, this local contact will never earn a dime for performing this service. It's part of leading by serving.

At Mary Kay they call that the "Go Give" spirit. The importance of this concept is recognized in the company's highest sales force honor. The annual Go Give Award recognizes those who best exemplify Golden Rule principles and the leadership virtues that were demonstrated so well by Mary Kay herself.

A look at successful leaders of other companies will reveal that they tend to have many of the same virtues. Yes, someone named "Chainsaw" or "Attila" occasionally comes along, cracks the whip, and enjoys short-term success. But long-term success tends to be reserved for people of character whose leadership style fits the six virtues.

Mary Kay lived by these ideals and spent a large part of her professional life teaching others to value them. That is why this book is dedicated to her and why she is likely to be remembered as one of the most effective CEOs ever to lead a company.

THE NINE KEYS TO SUCCESS

The first two chapters focused on the background of Mary Kay Inc. as well as the characteristics and practices of great leaders. The virtues of effective leaders described in Chapter 2 will serve any manager well. They are bedrock principles for personal success. Now we get to the question of sustainable success. What are the keys to achieving sustainable success? That is the question that will be answered in the remainder of this book.

I think there are nine keys. They have emerged out of studies of a number of truly successful companies. Almost across the board, it is clear that the companies that achieve sustainable success emulate these behaviors.

If you have read the first two chapters, you won't be surprised to learn that Mary Kay Inc. understands and practices the behaviors suggested by the nine keys. In fact, the company and its leaders do an exceptional job in this regard, and this consistent behavior leads to the kinds of results that others want to emulate. Mary Kay Inc. is one company that demonstrates by its practices how high performance can be achieved consistently over the long term.

3

Create and Maintain a Common Bond

As MARY KAY Inc. entered the new millennium, its leadership team realized that the company was beginning to lose some of the characteristics that had served it so well. Specifically, the corporate values and practices that created the common bond between all the employees, the independent sales force, and the organization's leadership appeared to be deteriorating.

This was an unwelcome discovery, but it was not swept under the rug—either then or now. All the executives with whom I spoke were quite forthright about the missteps of the company in the interval between the end of Mary Kay Ash's day-to-day involvement in the management of the firm as a result of her stroke in 1996 and Richard Rogers's return in 2001 as chairman of the firm.

Rogers's return signaled a return to the "Mary Kay way" of doing things: her values, practices, and commitment to managing by the Golden Rule. In fact, regaining that high ground—and using it to rebuild the common bond within the organization—became priority number one in 2001.

Richard Rogers hammered this home in his first remarks to both the sales force and the employees, reminding everyone that the name of the street that runs under the Mary Kay Building is Mary Kay Way.

And that, he said, "is the way it's going to be."

The Common Bond Drives Excellence in Performance

There are companies that create an attitude that goes far beyond just punching the clock and going home at the end of the day. They do that by creating a common bond. That bond is more than simple trust and integrity. It is a commitment among and between people that is ultimately a key aspect of the relationship between the company and its people. It is this bond that helps drive the performance of exceptional companies.

Skepticism Countered

A lot of companies talk a good talk when it comes to creating a common bond, but few walk the talk. Therefore, consultants, scholars, and others who make their way into the inner reaches of a company that talks a good talk are appropriately skeptical.

A first exposure to Mary Kay Inc. certainly provokes some skepticism. When one first hears Vice Chairman Dick Bartlett give an overview of company's internal operations, for example, it is hard to believe that any company could treat its people so well.

With skepticism fully engaged, therefore, I began this study of Mary Kay Inc. My first stop was at the desk of a woman named Gay Scoggins. Gay works as an executive assistant at corporate headquarters and deals with people from all over the world at all levels. She is well positioned to know a lot about how the company really works.

When one understands the psychological and financial rewards of being, say, one of the company's more than 200 Independent National Sales Directors, it is easy to understand why those people are very enthusiastic supporters of the company. It's not so obvious, though, why some-one like Gay, on the corporate side, would share that enthusiasm. After all, isn't a job just a job?

Not for Gay. She believes that she works for a value-driven organi-zation, and for her that's enormously rewarding. "You've got to under-stand," Gay explained. "These principles are not just some words on a plaque. This is *how we do business*. More than that, from your first day here you are fully aware of what is expected in everything from keeping the principles alive to dealing with members of our sales force. It's the same from the bottom to the top."

Gay confirmed that the Golden Rule and the values presented in the company's intensive new employee orientation are the standard of practice in the everyday operation of the company. She explained that every aspect of her own training has been tightly interwoven with the practices and principles of the firm.

Listening to her talk, you begin understand what she really experi-ences and values within the organization: a strong sense of a common bond and a shared purpose. It is clear that throughout her 10 years with the firm the strength of that bond has continued to grow.

And as you venture farther afield in Mary Kay Inc., which is by any measure a very large organization, you keep running across the same common bond, the same sense of shared purpose. It's true for individuals within the organization. It's equally true for the independent contractors who make up the sales force. And for the most part, the longer their expe-rience with the company, the stronger the bond.

Mary Kay Inc. is a different type of company. It is a company that seems to soar in the heavens at altitudes few companies manage to achieve. But it is not alone. In the case of almost every company that achieves sustainable growth and profit, you will find a unique relationship between the organization, as characterized by its leaders, and the people in the organization.

So What Is the Common Bond?

In Chapter 2, while looking at Mary Kay the person, we discussed the virtues of great leaders. Those virtues are humility, seeking the best for others, expecting excellence, integrity, impatience with the status quo, and an indomitable spirit.

Not surprisingly, leaders with these virtues hope and expect that their people will exhibit them as well. (People of integrity want people of integrity around them.) Living out these shared virtues in a community of like-minded people produces a special relationship. It is a relationship of trust, but it is more than that. It is a *common bond.* It is a relationship that is the starting point for any great company because it creates the potential for an organization that can accomplish extraordinary things. Mary Kay Ash consciously built that potential into the company she founded, and the current leadership strives to maintain this unusual legacy.

The fact is, not many companies achieve this special status. The reason is simple: While most managers want to work for people who exhibit the virtues listed above, they don't live those virtues themselves. They want to have the benefits of the Golden Rule, but they don't want to live it.

Every year books and periodicals come out with lists of companies that are recognized as exceptional places to work. Mary Kay Inc. has consistently been included on such lists. Not surprising is the fact that many of the companies on these lists are top performers in their industries. What *is* surprising is that senior executives at other companies seem to fail to make the connection between (1) how people are treated and (2) the fact that when you are ranked one of the "100 best companies to work for in America," what's being measured is the way you treat people. It's a *philosophy*, and great corporate performance grows directly out of that philosophy.

Why and how? For one thing, people love to work for a company that has the same values they do. They love the sense of joint commitment. They revel in the sense that there's a powerful bond that binds people together in a common enterprise. It's this bond—and the belief that stands behind it—that fosters success.

David Holl, president and chief operating officer of Mary Kay Inc., articulates some of the unique aspects of the company. "We try to make sure that we hire the right kind of people," he says. "We want 'out of the box' thinkers who have the ability to get along well with others. A lot of people might have trouble adapting to our culture. If they're into political and territorial issues, they simply do not fit into this organization. Such behavior destroys trust, and that's a cornerstone of this organization."

He emphasizes the fact that people within the company never stop trying to build trust. "We're not perfect," he explains, "but we realize that trust is the basis for our performance. It allows people to interact in the interests of our sales force and their customers. It's simply critical, and we won't allow that to be destroyed."

Holl worked for a number of other companies before joining Mary Kay. Almost from his first day on the job at Mary Kay he knew that this company was different in fundamental ways. "Astoundingly," he said as he pointed down the hall toward the other executive offices, "we care a great deal about each other. I've never worked at a company like that before."

This was a story that I was to hear from many different people in many different ways in the course of conducting research for this book.

How Much Is One Plus One?

Some years back the notion of synergy came into vogue. Synergy is what happens when, by putting building blocks together, you get something that is bigger or better than the sum of the parts. It's when one plus one equals three. Great songwriting teams (Rodgers and Hammerstein, Lennon and McCartney) are an obvious case in point. Championship sports franchises (Lombardi's Packers, Auerbach's Celtics) are another. Separately they don't produce at the same level at which they produce together. Thus, one plus one equals three.

When synergy occurs in the corporate environment, it at first appears to be a bit mystical. A group of companies in an industry may seem to be more similar than they are different, yet one will stand head and shoulders above the pack in terms of performance. What's going on here?

In my experience the exceptional company (and only the exceptional company) is getting the benefit of synergy. Deep pockets, patents, world-class manufacturing skills, contacts in high places, high-power marketing techniques—all are helpful, but none is likely to set a company apart for very long. (Even the tightest patent eventually expires or gets circumvented.) No, what creates synergy in a corporation over the longer term is the quality of the relationships that exist within the organization.

Think about how many people go to work every day with the sole goal of putting in their eight hours and going home again. Unless you believe that people are fundamentally lazy and unmotivated—and I don't, by the way—you have to ask, "Where did that attitude come from?" You could blame a person's coworkers, but pretty soon you'd be back to the same question: Where did the coworkers' attitudes come from?

The answer in both cases is that the employees' attitude tends to be *simply a reflection of management's attitude toward them.* At companies where management lives the six virtues that are manifested by (but certainly not limited to) Mary Kay Inc., you simply don't find a lot of people punching the clock. These companies have found a way to tap and reinforce their employees' intrinsic motivation. They have found a way to let the people in their organizations make one plus one equal three.

The Common Bond: Changed Attitudes

"I don't work for the company, I work for the union."

People who spend lots of time in companies, especially struggling companies, have all heard some version of this statement many times. It takes different forms in different settings: "I'm in it for the money." "I'm looking out for number one." "I'm only sticking it out until bonus time." The lyrics may change, but the unhappy tune remains the same.

After a while, if you visit enough companies, you can spot the symptoms of this disease as soon as you walk in the door. The alienation is almost palpable. Yet very often you find that the company's management is blissfully unaware of the problem. Or worse, you find that it is well aware of the problem but assumes that nothing much can be done about it.

I recently visited a well-known Fortune 100 company engaged in manufacturing. On the day of my visit there was an equipment malfunction on one of the manufacturing lines. As a result, a large piece of equipment fell off the line, almost crushing an employee who was standing nearby. Believe me, it was a close call.

Imagine my reaction to what happened next. The plant manager bustled onto the scene with a very worried look on his face. Even before he had come to a complete stop, he blurted out the question that was in the front of his mind: "How soon can you get this line running again?"

On another day at the same factory, I'm told, a worker had a heart attack, stopping the production line. More or less the same thing happened: They pulled him off the line, put him down on the floor, and paid him minimal attention while they got the line going again. In both instances there was no expression of concern for the endangered or suffering employee or for the emotions of anyone around him. Every signal that management sent out went in the same direction: "You employees are not particularly important to us. What matters is keeping the line going."

The employees of this firm are some of the highest-paid workers in the world. They get exceptional benefits. They also are some of the most militant union members to be found in the world today, striking at the drop of a hat and generally displaying a take-no-prisoners attitude toward management. By and large they can't wait for the end of their shift. They can't wait until they can retire and leave behind an environment that they consider overwhelmingly negative.

I often talk about this company. I don't hesitate to criticize the union, which is certainly guilty of greed and shortsightedness. (How long can this company continue in this vein? How long can these high-paying jobs be sustained?) Yet my real criticism is reserved for management—not only at this particular company but at others like it.

These companies get what they deserve. They get people who start their careers with great attitudes, but in a short time those employees simply want to "do their eight and go home." That, of course, is the opposite of synergy. These companies will never show up on lists of great places to work, and they are unlikely to show up on lists of high-performing companies either.

The Common Bond Creates Synergy

The U.S. Marines have it. So do the Navy Seals and the U.S. Army Green Berets. They are a *team,* and they never leave a teammate behind. If you are fortunate enough to become a member of one of these exceptional organizations, you are one of a very few special people. These special people develop a common bond over time. As they train together and work together, their commitment becomes deeper and deeper. Ultimately, relationships develop—deep friendships that are likely to last a lifetime.

That is the type of common bond that exists in the Mary Kay organization. These people do not leave their friends behind. Sometimes, to be sure, they have to drag them screaming and kicking to success, but they never leave them behind. They care for those who are sick. They do not tolerate mismanagement or a lack of integrity in dealing with members of the team. Ego trips are not welcome, and humility is expected.

That does not mean that every member of the team is not committed to win and to achieve excellence *as an individual.* As was noted earlier, excellence and the expectation of excellence start as individual virtues. What this means is that all the members of the team also are committed to the success of the team. The result is synergy. The common bond creates a momentum, a sense of purpose, that most other groups do not have.

What Happens When the Common Bond Deteriorates?

In the introduction to this book I noted that Mary Kay Inc., like every other company I know about, has had its share of problems. In the late 1990s, for example, a number of people associated with the company began to believe that there was a deterioration in the common bond between corporate headquarters and the independent sales force.

One of the groups that was extremely concerned about this trend was the Independent National Sales Directors, which is the top tier of the sales force. They are the most listened-to group in the company's universe, even more than the product consumer, who is listened to quite carefully. Anecdotal evidence suggests that the sales directors attempted to bring their concerns before senior executives more than once, without success. The message was finally heard loud and clear at a National Sales Directors' meeting on the East Coast in the late 1990s.

"It became abundantly clear that these leaders of the sales force, the people we valued the most, believed that we were at risk of abandoning some of the basics on which the company was founded," recalls Tom Whatley, president of global sales and marketing. "We were being hit pretty hard by our own people. The view was apparently fairly widespread."

To use the language of this chapter, what Tom Whatley and other executives were confronted with was the deterioration of the common bond. This was cause for great concern because the company views the independent sales force as the foundation of its success. Without their contributions, there would be no Mary Kay Inc. In a very real sense, the future of the company was at stake.

The problem clearly related to the organizational void left by Mary Kay's decreased involvement in the firm, a problem not atypical of strong founder-led firms. Mary Kay Ash had suffered a stroke in February 1996 that severely restricted her ability to speak, and as a result, much of her day-to-day involvement with the firm ceased. Even though she had become chairman emeritus of the firm in 1987, she had continued to make appearances, spend time in her office, and make her presence felt. After the stroke, the sense of security—and the steady reinforcement of the common bond—that came with her presence began to erode.

In response, the company tried a number of different management combinations—person X in job Y, person Y in job X, and so on—but none seemed to be just right. "We had some really great people who tried to take key roles," said Tom Whatley, "but it just did not seem to click. I would be the first to say that it was not their fault. It was just that the chemistry was not there."

Another piece of the puzzle began to emerge as well: Mary Kay's personal philosophy that corporate resources were to be focused on the development and support of thousands of microentrepreneurs in the sales force. This core belief was being diluted by corporate diversification efforts that were understandable in their own terms but inimical to the culture of the place. It was, recalls one manager who was close to the situation, a failure to recognize that Mary Kay Inc. is a *people* business rather than a collection of distribution channels.

But much of the solid foundation that the founder had laid remained intact. Enough people at the firm knew enough about Mary

Kay's principles to keep hammering away at them and eventually to help bring about a rekindling of purpose and principle. The overall goal was to regain the trust of the sales force, which would require a concerted effort. But this time the burden could not be placed on Mary Kay herself. As one person who was close to the process recalls, "Mary Kay was not able to speak, and so it became very clear that both the sales force and the company would collectively need to become her voice."

By June 2001, when Mary Kay's son and cofounder Richard Rogers once again took on the chief executive officer's role (in addition to that of board chairman), it was clear that it was only a matter of time before the firm's senior management team was composed of "homegrown" leaders and people with great admiration for Mary Kay's style of leadership. As a group, they clearly understood that they worked at a place that had a unique attribute, one that was a highly competitive advantage as well as a principled way of life. They also understood what was at risk when the common bond was damaged or diluted.

Revitalizing the Common Bond

With his own insight into the business—as well as financial prowess developed over more than three decades at the helm—Richard Rogers made it perfectly clear upon his return that he intended to continue the time-honored traditions of the company.

One thing that he and his colleagues soon realized was that a number of people at the company were *acting*, rather than *living*, its values. There was a great deal of attention paid to the "show" of things and to behaving in ways that were thought to be politically correct. These weren't necessarily mortal sins, but they certainly didn't stand in for the real thing. To the extent that energy and resources were going into acting rather than being, the company had a problem.

It quickly became apparent that what needed to happen was for the entire organization to return to living the values and principles, not just work at acting them out. "We decided to let the culture *be*," explains one of the most tenured of the executive team, Brad Glendening. "We let it be what it *was* rather than focusing on image and political correctness. What we know is that our sales force needs our support, our encouragement, and our advice. They don't need us to redefine what the Mary Kay culture teaches them. That is something they clearly understand."

Protect the Common Bond When Business Is Bad

For Mary Kay Inc., 1997 was an uncharacteristically flat year. Despite the fact that throughout the rank and file in the organization there were people who had performed in an outstanding manner, the company met almost none of its goals. What does the company do when things get rough?

"When we don't do well as a company," David Holl says, "we certainly don't take it out on those people who worked hard, did their best, and achieved their goals." And so in 1997 senior management took responsibility for the organization's poor performance. No one from the vice presidential level on up received bonuses. "Everyone else in the organization who achieved their goals got their bonus as promised," Holl explains. "It's all about the common bond."

Use the Internet to Support, Not Subvert, the Common Bond

During the 1990s direct-sales companies such as Mary Kay Inc. realized that they had to come to terms with a new, confusing, and much-touted technology: the Internet.

Among the members of the industry association, the Direct Selling Association (DSA), two very different responses to the Internet emerged. One camp feared the Internet as a disruptive technology and was inclined to ignore it and hope it would go away. The other camp plunged in with both feet, setting up Internet distribution and sales systems that promised improvements of 30 percent or more in profit margins. This certainly sounded attractive, except that this new channel would compete directly with those companies' independent sales forces and therefore might change the companies in ways no one could predict.

Both paths—do nothing and alter your business in fundamental ways—were risky. What did Mary Kay Inc. do? It looked for a third path.

"Rather than seeing the Internet as a way simply to increase our profits," recalls David Holl, "we saw it as a tool for strengthening the common bond within our organization." The company therefore developed an approach to the Internet that from day one focused on the needs of the Mary Kay Independent Beauty Consultant. The Internet would be used to support the independent sales force in any way possible. For example, a system was developed by which any customer could go online and order a product directly from her Independent Beauty Consultant at any time, 24 hours a day. If you were a new online customer and didn't yet have an Independent Beauty Consultant, you could type your home or office ZIP Code into a form and be given contact information for one living nearby. New online techniques were developed to complement the promotional efforts of the Independent Beauty Consultants. Finally, major resources were devoted to making the Internet a vehicle for faster and better communication between the company and its sales force.

It turns out that this sales force–oriented strategy was the right one. A 2000 ranking by *Interactive Week* placed Mary Kay Inc. in the top five worldwide for online sales in the retail sector. Mary Kay's online business has increased in the ensuing years. Today 70 percent of the U.S. sales force participates in Mary Kay's online programs.

Holl believes this phenomenal success is due to the fact that the Mary Kay Internet strategy dovetailed perfectly with the company's larger strategy. Both are related to maintaining the common bond. "Our manager's job," he says, "is to keep our people happy. I'm not talking about superficial things; I'm talking about things that matter, like being truthful, being encouraging, and helping them achieve more than they thought they could.

"Our Internet strategy has the same objective: We use this remarkable new tool to strengthen the common bond. Further, in order to build trust, there had to be no doubt in anyone's mind as to what our long-term plan was with regard to the use of the Internet. Thankfully, our trust relationship is such that we were able to carry out our strategy quite well."

A high-performing company builds on trust in ways that create more trust. The common bond is called upon and is reinforced.

The Care List, the Common Bond, and Tragedy

Company founder Mary Kay Ash took personal responsibility for reinforcing the common bond. At the peak of her business career she personally sent an average of 5,000 letters and cards each month. And she did not simply sign form letters; she directed a personal response to every individual. In many cases she would try to include something inspirational and personal, especially for people going through difficult times.

Over time this personal effort (and related activities) evolved into something called the care list. As Vice Chairman Dick Bartlett explains:

Mary Kay herself pioneered the care list concept, which was later adopted by every senior executive as a matter of routine. She developed a system whereby she heard weekly from every sales director about illness or tragedy within a unit and would then call or write an appropriate note of encouragement or condolence. Members of the sales group also performed this function, but the leadership team felt it was important to expand it to incorporate all senior management as well.

So every week, as they have done now for years, executives get on the phone with the care list in front of them to call those who are facing illness or personal tragedy. They make sure that this connection that goes beyond a simple business relationship is maintained. To them it is much more than a business relationship. It is a bond, a common bond of strength, care, and commitment that grows stronger every day.

Mary Kay is really an extended family, and by talking to those who are seriously ill, have lost a loved one, or have had some other family tragedy, we stay in touch with the very heart of our mission. Enriching women's lives is not just about money or material possessions but is really about caring, helping people through trying times, and, of course, celebrating their achievements as well. It's what a well-balanced family does instinctively.

The care list goes out each week to the members of the executive team, informing them of personal tragedies in the lives of Mary Kay employees and beauty consultants. In much the same way that Mary Kay herself did, executives devote time each week to writing and calling to encourage people in a crisis. Again, the care list is one way that the common bond connection is maintained even as the company grows, and it is considered one of the most important tasks in the workday of each executive.

A severe test of the Mary Kay "family" came on September 11, 2001, when the attacks on the World Trade Center and the Pentagon occurred. Not surprisingly in an organization the size of Mary Kay Inc., a large number of people associated with the company were touched personally by tragedy.

Some lost their lives. Carol Rabalais, an Independent Beauty Consultant in New York, was on the ninety-eighth floor of the World Trade Center. In the terrifying moments after the tower was hit Carol had only a few seconds to call her mother. "Please just take care of my children," she said. Then the line went dead.

As the news of Rabalais's death spread, the common bond that binds Mary Kay people became fully evident. Area sales force members—all independent entrepreneurs—joined to donate portions of their sales to the care of Carol's three children.

Genelle Guzman, a highly motivated performer in her part-time Mary Kay business, worked on the sixty-fourth floor of the World Trade Center for the Port Authority of New York. She was trapped on the thirteenth floor of her building, between giant slabs of concrete, for 26 hours after the attack. Genelle was the lone survivor from her office.

The Mary Kay family rose to the occasion. Comfort letters went out to each and every member of the sales force touched by this tragedy and in many cases to their family members as well. A tragedy relief fund was set up, corporate donations were made, and funds were disbursed to victims in December 2001.

Concluding Thoughts: The Common Bond

People want to care about their work. They want to believe that at the end of the day they have done something more than make money.

What do people talk about when they go home at night to their spouses and families? Sometimes they talk about the deals they closed or the money they made. More often they talk about the feeling of accomplishment they got when they helped another person. They talk about the friends with whom they get to work. They talk about the things that matter.

One of the Independent National Sales Directors I spoke with put it best: "I get to help other people, and along with that I get to make money. What better work could anyone have?"

It's *people*, united by a common bond, who make a high-performance organization. It's about getting the best from people by giving them the things they want the most in their lives. "This is about much more than selling lipstick," Mary Kay said on many occasions. "We are changing lives."

4

Create the Future: Think and Act Strategically

HERB KELLEHER, the chief executive officer who put maverick Southwest Airlines on the map, often talks about how his firm really does not have a corporate strategy. In fact, he sometimes claims that he does not believe in "strategy."

Those familiar with the company, however, understand that Southwest Airlines has a complex, far-reaching strategic plan. That is almost always true of excellent companies. The fact is, you can learn a lot about a great company by looking at its strategy.

Maybe you are tired of the "S" word and are tempted to tune out. Isn't strategy something that gets worked out at strategic retreats, captured in thick bound volumes, and then more or less ignored by a company that has to respond to a changing reality? Isn't strategy one of the things that everybody pays lip service to but (1) feels left out, (2) forgets about on a day-to-day basis, or (3) both?

The answer depends on the company. At Mary Kay Inc. everyone cares about strategy. That's the case in part because in one way or another almost everyone is involved in helping to create the firm's strategic plan. That means that they all have a *stake* in its fate.

Corporate strategy as it is normally practiced is a systematic process of discovering a firm's strengths and weaknesses, creating a mission statement, and going forward by "staying in the box." In other words, you compete where your firm has a competitive advantage and avoid realms in which others have a competitive advantage.

But a more sophisticated approach to strategy focuses on the *ends* rather than the means. Companies that set out to *win* (the ends) see their traditional core competencies as means to their ends. If you see an important capability or product that you want (or need), you first look for it within your organization. If it's not there, you *go get it.*

Mary Kay was explicit on this point. She believed that if others had an advantage that you didn't, your job was to find a way to correct that weakness. You have to build on your base but create excellent products or services for your target customers. If you can't do that today, *fix what's wrong.*

Powerful and compelling strategies are rarely the result of one person in the corner office cooking up a new scheme. Far more often great strategies are the result of focused teams asking and answering the key question: How can we be great in the future? Obviously, the more talented and committed people you have focusing on this question, the better off you'll be.

Strategy can be—should be—the *process of maximizing today and tomorrow.* It should be a plan for achieving excellence over the long run. Obvious? Unfortunately, it is not so obvious at lots of companies, including many whose names you'd recognize.

Many companies that get into trouble suffer from what Mary Kay called "quarteritis." That is, they are concerned mainly about the present. Exceptional companies are different. Yes, they keep their eye on the ball in terms of today's performance. At the same time, though, they're aware that the present has to be devoted in part to creating the profit potential of the future.

The past plays a role too, but as was implied above, one of the things that get companies into trouble is an excessive focus on their traditional core competencies. Companies that spend an inordinate amount of time looking backward and honing yesterday's skills can get into trouble quickly.

How is Mary Kay Inc. different? An outsider might suggest that the company has long been aware of and has focused on its core competencies: the production and marketing skills that have positioned it to be the premiere brand in the global cosmetics market. But in reality, as at other exceptional companies, at Mary Kay almost everything is changed continually. It is this *iconoclastic* mindset that keeps the company at the forefront of "anticipating customers' needs." To maximize both today and tomorrow, the company has had to become a master of change. It's a question of balance or, perhaps more accurately, of concurrent investments. While certain core values are maintained carefully, the concept of the firm's core competencies is abandoned so that every leader starts each day with a blank slate and a mission to focus on creating maximum value for the customer.

In conversations with David Holl, the company's president and chief operating officer, I gained some insight into the firm's strategic approach. It consists of five component parts: core cosmetics, international, leveraging technology, financial strength, and something called sustaining the soul. Let's look at each one in turn.

Core Cosmetics

One of the key insights that the company's leadership achieved a number of years ago was that the *company's products would change continually.* But that puts it a little too simply. More accurately stated, markets for cosmetics would evolve continually, and cosmetics would have to evolve along with them. Cosmetics would stay at the core, and there would be a nucleus of reasonably stable core products. Meanwhile, innovation would occur at the margins as the company pursued new opportunities.

For example, fairly early on Mary Kay's leaders spotted an interesting trend that seemed to be intensifying as the years went by: The daughters of current Mary Kay customers wanted to use the product. That meant that the firm had to be able to understand a rapidly changing younger market. Although this market by definition was relatively easy to reach, it wasn't necessarily easy to satisfy. Not only did these daughters have the same high expectations of the company's products that their mothers had, they also wanted products that were designed specifically for their own age group.

As a result, the company developed an entirely new line of products—the Velocity brand—intended to complement its core line and meet the needs of a younger market. Each year the Velocity offerings are modified to reflect the fashion season and changes in consumer preferences.

Meanwhile, of course, the classic lines in the skin-care product group remain more or less constant aside from the occasional addition. To restate the strategy principle offered above: Capitalize on today while preparing for new products and new markets tomorrow.

International

In most years the company has experienced double-digit growth, and the leadership team would like that trend to continue. But even though Mary Kay is among the best-selling cosmetics brands in the United States, the North American market is finite. This points to an increased emphasis on the international market in the company's most recent strategic plan.

As the company looks to new geographic markets, it has had to decide which of its core competencies must be re-created in other countries. One logical answer would be the world-class independent sales organization that the company has built over the years. Another would be the firm's demonstrated ability to anticipate market changes and senior management's related ability to deal with numerous "frame-breaking shifts"—discontinuities—in the global marketplace. Still another would be the research and development team's ability to continue creating products that meet consumers' evolving needs.

Get ready for what may be an unsatisfying answer to the question of what makes Mary Kay Inc. so successful that it must be re-created overseas: It's all of the above—the sales force, skilled leadership, product innovation, and more. Penetrating international markets requires bringing all these separate strengths to bear.

"This is one of the most complex companies on earth," observes Tom Whatley, who is responsible for global sales and marketing. All that complexity comes to bear on the challenge of becoming a global player.

By the measures that count most to the company, its international strategy has been successful. Market penetration and sales growth are critically important, and today Mary Kay cosmetics are sold in 33 key markets around the world. But also important is the number of lives that have been changed in positive ways.

This measure is necessarily anecdotal, but consider what one mainland Chinese woman recently said to a member of the Mary Kay corporate staff when explaining why she had chosen to affiliate with this particular U.S.-based cosmetics company: "I want to do something great with my life."

Once again we can see the core mission of the company—creating opportunities for women—surfacing in powerful ways. The internationalization of the corporate strategy, it turns out, is greatly facilitated by the power of the corporate mission statement, which appears to resonate in cultures around the world.

Leveraging Technology

Not all that many years ago Connie Lustig, a member of the Mary Kay independent sales force, lived her life entirely outside of cyberspace. Sure, there was a personal computer over in the corner that occasionally proved useful for a mundane task such as word processing. But Lustig didn't have Internet access and didn't want it. The truth was, she had no particular interest in technology and had no reason to become interested.

Then she was asked to participate in a Mary Kay pilot program. That program was conducted long before the Internet became a common business tool. As a result of the training she received in the program, she went from zero to 100 percent proficiency on her computer in a relatively short period of time and also made friends with the previously mysterious Internet.

Her new skills helped her business grow, and she soon got the use of a brand-new pink Cadillac. There was nothing unusual about that, except that when Lustig submitted the order for her new car, she made an off-beat request of Cadillac: She told the dealer that she wanted *two* cigarette lighters in the driver's console. The most curious thing was that Lustig was a nonsmoker. The explanation? She was a Mary Kay entrepreneur who wanted to run her office from wherever she was. At the time, the easiest way to get DC power in a car was to tap into the cigarette lighter socket. Lustig figured that with an extra DC outlet in her car, she'd find it easier to power her cell phone, laptop, and printer.

Today Lustig keeps her printer and a postage meter in the backseat of the Cadillac and her notebook computer and cell phone in the front seat. Using her mobile network connection, she prints out invoices, places orders, and sends e-mails from the road.

Lustig's personal journey symbolizes the technological journey of the organization. Throughout the 1990s Mary Kay Inc. wrestled with finding a way to add a rich technology component to the Mary Kay arsenal without sacrificing the people aspects that traditionally sustained the organization. At that time most Independent Beauty Consultants were not active on the Web. The company saw at least two good reasons to change that state of affairs. First, the independent small-business owners could only benefit from the kinds of information they could get from the Web. Second, they also would benefit from having an Internet presence of their own, especially one that was tied to the powerful marykay.com Web address.

At the same time, though, the company was inclined to move cautiously in this new realm. A lot of companies had already discovered that the "leading edge" of technology could quickly turn into the "bleeding edge." Many had already spent massive sums on technology, only to find that no one was interested in the result. To compound these companies' frustrations, those huge investments began to become obsolete before they could be brought on line.

Surveying this unhappy landscape, the Mary Kay leadership decided that the new technologies could indeed be a valuable business tool, but only if handled properly. At the same time they decided that those technologies would become widely accepted and adopted only if their value to the user was *obvious* and *compelling*. This was a tall order given the technological state of the art at that time.

To jump to the end of the story, Mary Kay today is recognized as one of the earliest successful adapters of high technology among bricks-and-mortar companies. Mary Kay Inc. not only has outpaced its industry peers, it also has managed to "work smarter" in the high-tech arena than many technology companies do.

How exactly did this happen? The firm employed a carefully orchestrated phase-in strategy, developing proprietary technologies and teaching the use of those technologies in a purposeful sequence, beginning with the top sellers. Here's the chronology:

1995   First Internet delivery of business reports to Independent Sales Directors

1998   First electronic ordering by Independent Sales Directors

1999   Web-order capability for Senior Consultants in the U.S. independent sales force

2000   Web-order capability for everyone in the U.S. independent sales force

Today more than three-quarters of all ordering revenue arrives online. In 2002 an estimated 3 million wholesale orders were placed online. Some 475,000 Independent Beauty Consultants in the United States are online. Approximately 125,000 Independent Beauty Consultants participate in the "Personal Web Site" program, which provides them with a customized Web site of their own, which their customers can use to shop online directly with them around the clock, seven days a week (24/7 in the lingo of high tech). The company hosts, maintains, and regularly refreshes the shared content of those sites. This keeps it up to date, ensures that each site reflects well on the Mary Kay brand, and of course makes Mary Kay products easily accessible to each consultant's customers.

In short, the Web has become what Chief Information Officer (CIO) Kregg Jodie calls "the artery of communication for Mary Kay today." Most people in the company attribute this success to a key decision at the outset: to use the Internet as a complement to existing channels rather than as a disruptive force. "We never seriously considered using the Internet to bypass our sales force," Jodie says. "It wouldn't fit our model. Our business is about our sales force, and our strongest competency as a company is our great network of people."

Notably, Mary Kay's common bond (see Chapter 3) made all this much easier. One interesting feature of the technology-adoption process at Mary Kay was that a large number of consultants announced that if Mary Kay was willing to "buy into" technology, so were they. It was a virtuous circle: The more people who logged on, the better the tool would be, and the more people who would log on.

Not that there hasn't been the occasional glitch. At one point, for example, the company decided to hold an online promotion that it dubbed a Founder's Day Sale. The trouble was that the sale created an online stampede. More than 100,000 Independent Beauty Consultants logged on at the very minute the sale was scheduled to start. As the seconds went by and as more and more people logged on to the system, the company's internal tech team began to get a sinking feeling: Perhaps we've underestimated demand here. It did not take long for their fears to be realized. About four minutes into the sale the system was overwhelmed, and traffic ground to a halt.

Good organizations learn from their mistakes, and this particular mistake happened only once. In short order the company adjusted the way online transactions were handled, and system capacity has increased steadily. In March 2002, for example, some 280,000 transactions came in via the Internet, with an average of 40 to 60 line items (i.e., separate orders) per transaction.

On the technology front, Mary Kay Inc. is in an unusual position. The company is supporting hundreds of thousands of people who are running their own businesses—businesses that need to be in close contact with the "home base." Each technological enhancement has to serve both purposes or at least not impede one while it advances the other. The Internet needs to be an opportunity creator in keeping with the corporate mission.

So far the strategy appears to be working. As CIO magazine recently concluded, "Mary Kay has found a way to foster its primary asset—an enthusiastic sales force—while harnessing e-commerce efficiencies."

Financial Strength

A third component in the company's strategic plan is *building and maintaining financial strength.*

First, some background: As was mentioned in previous chapters, money is the lifeblood of business. Every company above a certain size spends a good deal of time (and money) worrying about money. In most cases these worries boil down to two issues: (1) Are we making money? and (2) Is our cash flow adequate to meet our day-to-day needs?

Both questions circle back to an underlying issue: the capitalization of the company (this refers to the source of the money that underlies the company's operations). There are lots of places to go for operating capital, but it mostly boils down to three main options: (1) bring your own to the table (as Mary Kay Ash did in 1963 with her hard-earned $5,000) and keep adding to that stake with reinvested profits, (2) sell stock in the company, and (3) borrow money. In the real world, of course, most companies wind up resorting to all three, either one at a time or in combination.

Each option has pros and cons. Self-funding is a wonderful thing, but in most cases your own stake is limited, and if your company is successful, it can outgrow that initial stake quickly. Selling stock, of course, brings all the complications associated with regulators and shareholders, who may have expectations of the company that cramp its operating style. Borrowing—something we're all familiar with in the personal realm— also can be good or bad. By borrowing, a company with $1 million net worth can act like a company with $5 million of equity. Not surprisingly, most companies today are leveraged—in debt—to some extent. But being in debt, as we all know, also has disadvantages.

In 1968, five years after its founding, Mary Kay Inc. took the sale-of-stock route. That strategy enabled the company to expand beyond the capital it could amass as a privately held company and also helped it avoid the risks associated with borrowed funds. In 1985, a little less than two decades later, Mary Kay Inc. went back to the future, paying out nearly $400 million to buy back all the publicly held stock in the company. The reason was straightforward: Neither Mary Kay nor her son believed that it was possible to run the company in the best interests of the organization and also meet the demands of Wall Street.

The buyback freed Mary Kay Inc. from the tyranny of Wall Street, but since much of the capital needed to buy back the company was borrowed capital, this meant that the company was once again in a position of being leveraged. (In this lingo of this trade, this is a leveraged buyout, or LBO.) Yes, there were risks involved, principally the fact that the company couldn't generate the cash flow needed to service the debt. As it turned out, this wasn't a serious problem. The company paid down its debt over time and also invested in long-term strategies that would enhance the growth and profitability of the firm significantly, all without having to pay out dividends to investors.

The plan worked. It is a testimonial to the financial acumen of the organization that since 1985 it has been able to grow into a $1.4 billion-plus at wholesale ($2.8 billion at retail) organization without infusions of public capital.

In developing the firm's strategic plan in 2001 the management team decided to add a key piece to the long-term strategy: *Enhance financial strength.* To most astute observers this would have been a puzzling priority indeed. In light of its sales growth, the company was already minimally leveraged. What did Mary Kay's leaders mean by "financial strength"? They meant "getting out of debt." The company's management decided to go against the common business wisdom and become a debt-free company. Mechanisms are now in place to accomplish that goal, which, if achieved, will put the company back in the position it enjoyed back in the earliest days of the founding era. Of course, the company will be immeasurably stronger. This will benefit all those associated with the company and position the company to take full advantage of new opportunities as they present themselves.

Sustaining the Soul

As was explained in the last chapter, the problems of the late 1990s revealed that one of the most serious risks the company faces is forgetting its roots. Mary Kay Ash spent her entire working life making sure that the practices and principles of her firm would not be forgotten. Unfortunately, her determination alone wasn't enough to make those teachings stick indefinitely.

With the help of a forceful wake-up call from the independent sales force, as was described in earlier chapters, management realized that it had allowed the company to begin drifting away from its philosophical roots. This realization caused an internal examination that in turn led to a new strategic push.

The goal of this new push is to reinforce management's commitment to the firm's founding principles. It is to remind corporate management and sales force leaders that they are the "keepers of the flame," in other words, responsible for sustaining the company's practices and principles. Core values can't be left to chance; they have to be nurtured and protected.

This is especially true in an industry that is fiercely competitive, in which everything is changing constantly and the pace of change is accelerating. Any company that ignores its context is doomed to failure, of course, and leading is always better than following. "The speed of the leader is the speed of the gang," Mary Kay Ash wrote in her book.[1] But there will inevitably come circumstances in which expediency—the easy way to meet the needs of the moment—must give way to principle. Management has to be skilled in spotting those circumstances and courageous enough to do the right thing when they arise.

I happened to see one such decision point. I was interviewing a Mary Kay executive, and an associate interrupted our meeting with a pressing problem. (This was unusual in my experience of the company.) I stayed, more or less as a fly on the wall. After the two managers discussed the issues, they concluded that there was only one decision that they could make. "We have to go with our values," said one. The other concurred. They both seemed confident that they had made the right decision even though the path they had chosen was not without risk. They had invoked the underlying values and principles that had always served as the foundation for the company's long-term success, and that was very likely to be the right decision.

Strategic Principles

Dick Bartlett says that while corporate strategy may change, the firm's "strategic principles" must be unchanging. It is the firm's strategic principles that allow it to be highly fluid, adaptive, and competitive. Those principles establish the framework on which corporate flexibility is established.

One of the challenges typically faced by direct-sales organizations is a lack of trust between the field sales organization and the corporation. In these cases the field sales agents are convinced—rightly or wrongly—that the corporation is determined to obtain the names of the customers of the independent sales agents and then bypass those agents, selling directly to the customers. The short-term result would be higher profits to the corporation as the "middleman" was cut out. (The longer-term result, of course, would be a different story.) There have been enough incidents in the direct-sales field to justify these kinds of suspicions.

Unfortunately for both the corporation and the field sales organization, these suspicions rule out a whole range of tools and tactics that otherwise would be helpful to both partners. That's why Mary Kay Inc. has worked hard to build and protect a firm foundation of mutual trust to improve the competitive position of both the corporation and the field sales organization.

The results have been very positive. A number of years ago, for example, the Mary Kay organization realized that it had the ability to provide a well-rounded suite of marketing services that would help streamline and bring benefits to its Independent Beauty Consultants. The proposed program was called Direct Support. Later it became known as the Preferred Customer Program.

The program featured a high-quality, professionally produced custom mailing to every Mary Kay "preferred customer." It drew upon the company's research and development (R&D) activities and increasingly sophisticated technology infrastructure and also took advantage of its bulk printing and centralized advertising services to produce a cost-effective advertising product. Significantly, it came to each customer as a personalized mailing from that customer's Independent Beauty Consultant. For mere pennies per customer, in other words, the consultant could deliver periodic product offerings and keep her customers abreast of fashion trends, new products, and seasonal updates. Participation in the program was completely voluntary.

Where others had failed, Mary Kay Inc. was successful. The reason, simply put, was *trust*. The company's Independent Beauty Consultants had confidence that their customer lists would not be stolen or abused in any way. They believed that the company's plan had been conceived for their mutual benefit, and that confidence proved to be well placed: The Preferred Customer program has been extremely successful. (It has become even more so as it has become integrated with the larger Internet outreach and communications effort.) Sales figures show that the sales consultants who chose to participate enjoyed increased business success.

The point is that trust creates opportunities and that trust grows out of consistent and principled behavior.

Don't Rest on Your Laurels

Mary Kay Ash often commented that "a laurel rested upon becomes wilted."

Her pointed observation, tinged with humor, was intended to keep her company on guard against complacency: the silent killer of successful companies. No matter how good you are today, that probably won't be good enough tomorrow. Get ready for change. *Embrace* change.

Mary Kay Inc. is a nearly continuous success story over almost four decades but consider the enormous changes that lie behind that seeming continuity. Women hadn't yet entered the workforce in large numbers in the 1960s, but Mary Kay found ambitious and talented women who wanted to get out of the house and do something great with their lives. The result? A Cinderella success story, in part because by the 1970s many working women were encountering glass ceilings and finding out how difficult it was to be a full-time mother and a full-time wage earner. Mary Kay provided a third option, and it appealed to a wide range of women.

But hard economic reality continued to drive many women into the full-time workforce. The result? By the 1980s there were far fewer women at home during the day to host skin-care classes and product demonstrations. A change in tactics was called for, conceived, and implemented. The result again was success, although this time success had a different face.

Internationalization, the Internet, and other fundamental economic changes also forced strategic change at Mary Kay Inc. Through the 1990s and into the new century the company has been able to evolve, morph, and change almost continuously.

At the same time, *principle prevails.* The company scrutinizes itself for its adherence to time-honored principles and practices and, although intensely focused on opportunity, ignores opportunities that don't sit comfortably within the corporate value system.

Yes, it is a difficult balancing act, but sustaining principles provide the safety net.

Note

1. Mary Kay Ash, *Mary Kay on People Management.* New York, Warner Books, 1984.

5

Make Me Feel Important!

THERE IS ONE thing, above all else, that is critical in the creation and operation of a company that has sustainable success. It's the thing that makes the difference between *good* and *great*. It's the thing that makes the difference between a few good years and many great years. At the same time, it is one of the most difficult things to accomplish.

It is the issue of *how people are treated.*

Something almost magical happens when people are treated well. When people feel valued and appreciated, they are more productive. The company is more competitive and is in a better position to treat its people well, and so on and so on. It's a virtuous circle.

Yet treating people well is surprisingly uncommon in corporate America.

Mary Kay Ash used to advise her colleagues that they should think of every person around them—superior, subordinate, peer, field sales representative, mail carrier, whoever—as having a sign around her or his neck that said, "Make Me Feel Important."

But many people in business take the opposite approach. They treat others as if they're wearing the sign around their necks. They're announcing to the world that they expect to be made to feel important. Subordinates in particular are expected to act this way. After all, the reasoning goes, aren't I paying that person pretty well? Shouldn't that guy who owes me his job cater to me?

Let's be honest: We all want to feel important. The question is how we achieve this elusive end, and there are two basic paths for getting there. One is to build up our own importance or significance at the expense of others. The other is to make the people around us feel more confident, more competent, and more valued.

A funny thing happens when you take the time to value others: They conclude that *you* are important (not to mention wise enough to recognize their merits). They perceive you as a caring individual. If they happen to be customers, their decision to do business with you is reinforced. If they happen to be your subordinates, they want to give more than 100 percent because they are motivated by your attitude and want to live up to the expectations of someone they respect.

An associate and I developed a leadership assessment that we have used at a number of companies. It measures how managers treat their subordinates. As a general rule, managers who receive low scores tend to be control-oriented people who rarely recognize a job well done. Managers who receive high scores tend to be people who clearly communicate their esteem for their people.

The low-scoring managers have little support within the organization. They have a hard time recruiting skilled people and therefore have a hard time getting difficult things done, or at least done right. The high-scoring managers, by contrast, usually have a waiting list of excellent people who want to transfer to their areas. And guess what: On a consistent basis, the high-scoring managers also have the highest-performing units.

A lot of people simply do not understand what happens at high-performing companies. They are confused or put off by the sheer enthusiasm that they see at work in these contexts. They are inclined to use words like *cult* to explain away high performance. Yes, there are people— and in some cases whole organizations—who take advantage of people's natural inclination to work hard and do their best. But organizations like this are relatively rare and don't last very long. The truth is, most people are pretty smart about people. It doesn't take long for people to see through such manipulative behavior. Then, once again, they'll be looking for an organization that will agree to value them.

Unwelcome Behavior Is Not Welcomed by Excellent Leaders

A prospective executive interviewed at Mary Kay Inc. a while back. He lived on the East Coast, and so the Mary Kay travel group helped arrange his trip to Dallas for the final interviews. But in dealing with the travel team and other support groups at Mary Kay, the man was abrasive, demeaning, and downright rude.

He came to Dallas and went through a series of interviews with various members of the executive team. At the end of his time in Dallas the consensus was nearly unanimous: He had done exceptionally well in his interviews. But the supervisor of the travel group was concerned. She felt strongly that the senior executives needed to know about the other side of this man's behavior. She called a senior executive to inform him of the problems her colleagues had encountered. End of story: No offer was made. "We don't hire people who treat others like that," said one executive.

The Thin Pink Line: Creating Unity of Purpose

Over the years I have had the opportunity to work with a variety of law enforcement agencies. At one point in my career I even worked as a chaplain for a local police department, and that involved attending the police academy and working as an officer at the department on my days off. In the course of this work I learned about what law enforcement officers call the "thin blue line," the ranks of law enforcement officers who stand between civilization and chaos. The phrase hints at the tough, confusing, and sometimes life-threatening situations police officers face. The result is a special camaraderie with and respect for each other. It involves a level of interpersonal commitment and support that rarely is seen in the corporate world.

But there are companies that try to build and foster that kind of mutual commitment, in large part by making people feel important, and Mary Kay is clearly one of those companies. Through hard work and consistent behavior the company creates what might be called the "thin pink line." Many, many members of the larger organization—extending to the members of the independent sales force—describe a connection and a bond with colleagues and the company that is not unlike that of a family. In literal terms they talk of "coming to each other's rescue," as in the cases of the sales director who rescued a colleague's daughter who was stranded on a boat during a hurricane and the sales director who received a call from a colleague to help a friend who had ended up in the hospital in that sales director's hometown.

In my work with law enforcement I noticed that more often than not police officers who decide to leave the profession find themselves longing to return to the job. Why? Because they *miss* the thin blue line. They miss the support and unconditional acceptance they found in police work.

People in the Mary Kay sales force often discover to their surprise that this unconditional acceptance and sense of being appreciated is one of the most treasured aspects of their business. True, the money—and the sense of personal satisfaction that comes with financial success—can be great. But even more important is the opportunity to work with people who honestly value you and think you are important.

The thin pink line may be too defensive a metaphor. The sense of comradeship and mutual support that prevails at Mary Kay is in fact a competitive advantage. It gives people confidence and encourages them to achieve at a higher level. People value their association with this company and therefore want to do well.

In fact, they want to do their absolute best.

Communicating Value Changes Lives

As I was researching this book, I became interested in how Mary Kay Inc. puts "valuing others" into practice. At my request, management asked the top Independent National Sales Directors in the company—known as the Inner Circle—to reflect on how this aspect of the company had had an impact on their lives. Following are excerpts from those stories:

- Pat Fortenberry talked about the riches that have come from "developing a positive attitude and passing it on. Not only did I pass this Mary Kay principle on to my Mary Kay family but to my own children . . . and this has impacted the lives of our grandchildren, who both have cystic fibrosis and still have positive attitudes."

- Joanne Holman spoke of "the common bond" as her most valued Mary Kay commodity: "It is a closeness that transcends even family ties. We've built businesses, raised families, celebrated successes, and grieved over loss together. Mary Kay believed that camaraderie could exist even among competitors. I am stronger because of this bond."

- Mickey Ivey, who is married to a minister, described Mary Kay as a "vehicle by which I could tremendously improve the lifestyle of my family, see so many other women believe in themselves and reach their true God-given potential. I did not have to sacrifice any of my beliefs or principles to attain the pinnacle of success this company offers."

- Emily McLaughlin found that "I have been able to develop my career through the various seasons of my life, beginning with three young children who needed my time and energy. Still I could build a strong foundation. Now, after 31 years, I'm able to feel the fulfillment of success without feeling that I have compromised my values."

- Marlys Skillings said that "especially now, our children need us to be there for them in a society where ethics and values depend on circumstances and situations." She says she values that far more than she did the modicum of celebrity she enjoyed hosting a television talk show. "The best part of Mary Kay principles," she writes, "is passing them on to others."

- Cheryl Warfield said that "living your life by the Golden Rule sounds so simple, but it's another thing altogether to live that way in the work environment. We find fulfillment and reward by living by the principles Mary Kay founded this company with." Her work helped her husband take early retirement at age 44 from his career as a bank executive.

- Karen Piro spoke about another of Mary Kay's principles, that of "spreading sunshine and love to all those around you. She taught us to be 'energy givers' to everyone, and as we pass these principles along to our children, we can positively impact the world."

- Christine Peterson has been greatly affected by Mary Kay's teaching her to value each person: "Mary Kay said we should pretend everyone wears an invisible sign that says 'Make Me Feel Important.' "

- Nancy Sullivan saw that principle in action as Mary Kay stood in the lobby of a busy hotel speaking one on one with her husband: "People were clamoring all around her, but Mary Kay never took her eyes off Dave. She also taught us that God never made a nobody, and that has helped me eliminate prejudice in dealing with people."

These are impressive testimonials, but there is one story among the Inner Circle—that of Kathy Helou—that seems to best capture the spirit of "make me feel important" at Mary Kay Inc. It's an almost unbelievable tale. Helou had been trying to climb the corporate ladder when she hit the glass ceiling, leading to an emotional crash that landed her in a psychiatric hospital for 40 days and put her on corporate leave for a year. While she was convalescing, she decided to become a contestant on *The Price Is Right*, a popular TV game show. She did well and almost won a car but instead ended up with a consolation prize: a computer and a collection of Mary Kay skin-care products. Although disappointed, Helou became intrigued by the noncomputer part of her consolation prize. To make a long story short, in the early 1990s she became the first Independent Sales Director to break the $2 million earnings barrier in unit sales in one year, a feat achieved by only two others since then. She recently wrote about this life-changing experience:

"Mary Kay was a defining moment where the entire trajectory of my life was altered by a culture so foreign to me at the time. This culture of 'doing unto others as you would have them do unto you' wasn't something I learned at the Fortune 100 company where I had worked before. There we learned survival skills—with many walking wounded from the scars of those battles.

"Winning that set of products turned out for me to be a way to learn life skills I lacked. Today my passion is to find women and be their encourager, to be a lifter and not a leaner. My goal is to help women elevate their self-esteem and self-worth, to know they are special. It is very clear that with Mary Kay you don't need a significant title to perform a significant role."

As with so many of the stories in the Mary Kay organization, there is more to Helou's story than just the transformation of a single individual's life. "This culture," she says, "is one that you can pass from generation to generation. You can adjust to it without compromising your values. We thank Mary Kay for the legacy she has left us."

Valuing Others: It's About Performance

Above all, Mary Kay Ash understood how important it is to be *valued*. As was noted in Chapter 1, she spent years achieving exceptional results, only to be overlooked by her superiors. Despite 25 years as a stellar performer in the direct-selling business, she was undervalued principally because she "thought like a woman." (The phrase sounds almost quaint today.) She missed promotions, not to mention income opportunities, simply because she was not a man.

She resolved that to the extent that it was in her power to do so, she would make sure that every person in the organization—male or female, young or old, highly educated or self-schooled—was valued. This commitment, born of adversity, became the foundation for everything Mary Kay did.

Mary Kay liked to tell the story of the young boy who finished in the lower half of his class. When asked about his class rank, he proudly announced, "I'm in the half that makes the top half possible." Ever the "possibility thinker," Mary Kay Ash would always challenge people in the lower half—gently but firmly—to set a new goal, to keep trying, and to come back the following year with a more positive story to tell. And in many cases they did.

Mary Kay also used humor to make her point while still making others feel important. Humor not only relieves whatever tension or anxiety may be in the air, it also helps communicate the idea of equality—the *team* focus—to others.

On one occasion, for example, Mary Kay was speaking with a group of employees, including a number of men who drove trucks for the company. She announced, poker-faced, that senior management had decided that all truck drivers would henceforth wear new pink jumpsuits with the Mary Kay logo on the back.

As one can imagine, this elicited an immediate and overwhelmingly negative response from the drivers. "We'll be laughed out of every truck stop from here to Los Angeles if you do that," they protested. "How could you *do* that to us?"

At that point she could no longer keep a straight face. Through her laughter, she admitted that no such action had ever been considered and that she certainly had no intention of doing such a thing. It went without saying, she quietly pointed out, that the company would never make a decision like that without seeking their input. As she had anticipated, the prank was well received—at least after the truckers got the image of themselves in the pink jumpsuits out of their minds. The fact that she took the time to play a practical joke on the fleet managers and drivers meant a great deal to them and gave them something personal to associate with her as their chief executive. It underscored the fact that she valued them. The story is still told around the company today, many years after it occurred.

And yes, the Mary Kay truck fleet *is* pink. Its truckers get waves and honks all across America, and they are, presumably, happy to walk into their favorite truck stops not dressed in pink.

Valuing People Means Trusting People

Let's go a little deeper into what it means to value people. It means that you *trust* them. By involving staff personnel in the most important aspects of the business, you send an unmistakable signal that you have confidence in them, and you give them a chance to see *how* they are valuable to the company. Finally, you give them an opportunity to see how other people in and around the organization are important. Involving others in decision making sends a clear message of trust and confidence.

It's a bit counterintuitive, but in many cases, as organizations grow, people get fewer opportunities to see why they are personally important to the company. People in staff roles, for example—where most of the workday is focused on more abstract managerial or functional duties isolated from the independent sales force and the end consumer—can get isolated and out of touch.

One effective countermeasure is to arrange to put staff members in direct contact with their "customers," the independent sales force. Vice Chairman Dick Bartlett explains:

> *In this regard, we recognize the value of periodic field sales force events. Our year starts with a "Leadership Conference" that brings together almost 10,000 of the top sales leaders at one conference location, which is an ideal venue to assign "support staff" not only to help out but to build their own relationships with the field sales force. Corporate staff members also help organize and support spring meetings called Career Conferences. In 2002, 70,000 members of the independent sales force attended some 40 Career Conferences.*
>
> *In order to contribute, volunteering support staff members have to learn new skills that often are far removed from their daily assignments, a cross-disciplinary training that in many cases proves valuable in the career development of the individuals involved.*
>
> *And then, of course, there's our most famous field independent sales force event: our annual Seminar, with almost 50,000 attending one of five back-to-back events in Dallas each year. Again, this provides an important interaction opportunity for the support staff. At the Seminar we make good use of "expo" formats, called "Idea Exchanges," where staff members man booths, answer questions, and demonstrate new products*

*or services or systems in person to the sales organization. Obviously, the idea exchange is two-way. All of this may be described as a giant, ongoing "service learning system," which is in reality based on our Mary Kay mantra—*Listen, listen, listen!

One of the great things about listening, of course, is that the people you listen to are eager to share their best ideas with you because you have demonstrated that you value them.

Where in the World Is Eden Prairie, Minnesota?

The conventional wisdom has it that to be a success in direct selling, you need to be located in a large market with large numbers of potential customers. A sales agent in the middle of nowhere therefore would have a built-in excuse for not producing: There aren't enough prospects in my territory.

But as the old saying goes, "Losers have excuses, and winners have reasons." Arlene Lenarz is one person who does not believe in excuses.

Lenarz, an Independent Executive National Sales Director, knows where Eden Prairie, Minnesota, is because she lives there. She is living proof that the size of the market is limited mainly by the boundaries of one's mind.

Her start with Mary Kay was a quiet one, but that was the last quiet moment in her career. She was a skilled and valued nurse, but the combination of four children and night and weekend shifts convinced her that her career was not in the best interest of her family. With the encouragement of her husband, she quit her nursing job and became a full-time mom.

Her first invitation to a Mary Kay event promised to be, as she recalls, a "ho-hum" experience. A Mary Kay Independent Beauty Consultant invited her, and Lenarz decided to go mainly because she was getting bored with watching *As the World Turns.*

Lenarz's story closely resembles those of tens of thousands of others who have decided to start a Mary Kay business. Yes, she loved the product, but what really hooked her was the environment. "Everyone there radiated from within," she recalls. "Their enthusiasm was contagious." In addition, she had been doing some thinking. The close spacing of her four children meant that the family was likely have four children in college at the same time. That is when she started looking for a way to supplement the family income. Needless to say, when she discovered Mary Kay Cosmetics, she had found a home.

When she told her husband that she wanted to start a part-time career as an Independent Beauty Consultant for Mary Kay, he made a point of saying that it would be "her" business as opposed to "their" business. That was his way of saying that it was all right for her to do this as long as he did not have to get involved. According to Lenarz, that attitude changed when it came time to start putting the checks in the bank and she asked her husband to make the deposits. He became increasingly enthusiastic as he realized the magnitude of her accomplishments, certainly including the money but extending beyond the money to her professionalism and sense of satisfaction.

Lenarz started her business in 1972 after taking time off from her nursing career so that she could care for her children. Just 12 months after setting up her business she had already created a 41-person unit and achieved the rank of Independent Sales Director. The next year hers was the sixth best performing unit in the country.

A time line of her progress in her Mary Kay business reveals the scale and scope of her accomplishment:

1972   Independent Beauty Consultant
1973   Independent Sales Director
1977   Independent National Sales Director
1994   Independent Executive National Sales Director
1996   Number One National Sales Director in the nation
       (first year attained)

By her reckoning, she has earned something in excess of $10 million in commissions since beginning a Mary Kay business. She has been the number one National Sales Director in the nation five separate times.

According to Arlene Lenarz, the problem with many people today is that they "won't inconvenience themselves for success." She hates to see a capable person walk away from a fulfilling life. At the same time, Lenarz loves to see others succeed. She believes that her responsibility is to focus on the value of others and help them realize what they are truly capable of doing. She believes that the ability to identify the special gifts of others is very important in helping them achieve their personal potential.

"It's really simple," says Lenarz, "Before Mary Kay I was petrified if I was asked to make an announcement at our PTA meeting. I did not believe that I was capable of doing a lot of things. Mary Kay changed all of that." As evidence of the transformation she went through, Lenarz recalls how she felt about the first five skin-care classes she held as a new beauty consultant: "The only way I can describe the way I felt when doing my first class is that I was *scared*," she says, smiling. "But by the time I got to my fifth, I was obnoxious. I had found a home and loved every minute of it."

This raises an interesting question. Who was more important to whom? Clearly, the company was lucky to get an individual like Lenarz, who has proved herself to be one of the best in the nation—or, indeed, the world—at what she does. But Lenarz puts it the other way around: "Mary Kay didn't need me," she says. "I needed Mary Kay."

And what did she need from Mary Kay? Belief in herself, which came from the company's belief in her. "It also became very clear to me," Arlene Lenarz says, "how important it is that Mary Kay believed in people. I have discovered that that's the key to leadership."

"Make Me Feel Important" Changes People

There was another event that changed Arlene Lenarz's life. The call came in 1974, from Mary Kay Ash herself, asking Lenarz to speak at the annual Seminar.

Frankly, Lenarz recalls, her first reaction was fear. When she expressed reservations about getting up in front of 7,000 people, Mary Kay patiently explained that the people coming to the Seminar needed to hear from someone exactly like her.

"All kinds of people are drawn to Mary Kay," Lenarz explains. "Of course, some are accomplished professionals who are looking for a different life for their children. But others, you might say, are from the fringe."

The second group, Lenarz continues, consists of women who come into the organization with extremely low levels of self-esteem. It is these people, she believes, who are likely to be changed the most—and benefit the most—from the Mary Kay experience. But the organization simply provides the *opportunity* for change, Lenarz emphasizes; the change itself has to come from within. She says she is always careful to explain to new members of the independent sales force that their lives and destinies are in their own hands. Unlike the promises of some of the pyramid-type companies, she says, Mary Kay places the focus on personal sales and a commitment to excellence.

"I explain that they have the ability to be making more than the governor of their state if they choose to do it," she says. "I explain that they can earn the use of a Cadillac and show how they can earn the position of Independent National Sales Director. You can't plant ambition in people; they have to do that for themselves. And once they're ready, it's their job from that point forward."

Lenarz tells the story of a new Beauty Consultant who was in her sales unit. The woman was divorced and had two young children. She was working as a hairstylist out of the basement of her home to provide for her two young children. She had no car and no money to buy products, but she did see the opportunity that Mary Kay offered. Her Independent Sales Director believed in her so much that she personally paid for the woman's initial inventory. Her faith in the young woman proved to be well founded. Seven years later the former hairdresser was an Independent National Sales Director with a six-figure income. All that was accomplished because someone believed in her and made her feel important.

Recognizing the value of people is key to understanding the success of the independent sales force. Certainly, its ranks include extraordinary people, but in most cases these are ordinary women with extraordinary desire. They want to win, and they want to be valued. The two goals and the ways they are attained are inextricably linked.

A Performance Lesson Learned

The general manager of one of the most prestigious hotels in New York once talked with a member of his staff about his personal experience of

Mary Kay Ash. This was an individual who was not easily impressed, but he admitted that he always was aware when Mary Kay Ash was visiting his hotel. The difference in the attitude among the staff was palpable, and her impact on a crowd was unique.

"You know," he told his colleague, "we deal with some of the most important people in the world at our hotel: the heads of countries, accomplished artists and musicians, and corporate CEOs. I have to tell you, I have never seen anyone move a crowd like Mary Kay Ash. There was simply something about her ability to make contact with others that touched everyone; each one of thousands in our hotel ballroom felt connected."

As with so many such stories at this company, there is more. The hotelier saw what happened in the ballroom but wasn't there later as Mary Kay was leaving the hotel. As an employee traveling with her tells it, Mary Kay noticed a woman in a wheelchair off to the side of the lobby ballroom where Mary had just spoken. She noticed that the woman was wearing a Mary Kay pin. Breaking through her security cordon and forgetting about her very tight timetable, Mary Kay Ash walked over to shake hands with the woman. No one asked that individual how she felt about being recognized—picked out of a crowd—by a business legend, but it's not difficult to guess.

I have witnessed senior executives fighting to get recognized and carrying those fights into the offices of key customers. It's not an exaggeration to say that I've seen companies destroyed by issues of recognition.

Why all this blood drama? People crave recognition. Through her simple act of walking over to express her support for and interest in the woman in the wheelchair, Mary Kay demonstrated what real leadership is all about. It is *not* about fighting to see who gets the credit. It is about realizing that by making others important, you become a leader.

People who live out "make me feel important" in the lives of others are the ones who foster excellent performance for an organization. They are the unselfish individuals who live out the Golden Rule in the lives of others.

Perhaps Arlene Lenarz put it best as she addressed the 2001 Seminar:

I was blown away at the first Mary Kay success meeting that I attended. My Mary Kay Beauty Consultant stood up to crow about her sales, her bookings, and her guest (me), and everyone cheered and applauded. I thought to myself, This is weird. I mean, what are they so excited about? See, we didn't do that at the hospital when someone got paid. But I soon discovered that being recognized and appreciated for exceptional work is really a reward in itself and that in Mary Kay encouragement is a gift that we give each other! Oh, what a life!

So many people are looking for some fun in their lives, and it's a fact that people rarely succeed in their work unless they have fun doing it. Well, we have more fun working than most people have playing. My Mary Kay work has always been play with a purpose. Of course, we take the business seriously, but we don't always take ourselves so seriously. When we learn to laugh at ourselves, one thing is for sure: We never run out of things to laugh at.

What They Don't Teach You at the Harvard Business School . . . or Anywhere Else . . . and Why It Is So Important

The best business schools in the world teach students all about finance, management, and corporate strategy. Yet with rare exceptions, most don't teach students about the most important leadership issue of all: how valuable making people feel important is when it comes to organizational performance.

We often forget that many of the practices in companies send exactly the wrong message. We foster cultures in which management spends a lot of time telling instead of listening. We separate senior executives from the people who do the work. We also make sure that the people who are identified as being the most important in a company are those at the top.

The truth in many cases is that it's *not* the people at the top of the organization who do the work that allows a company to achieve excellence. The most important people in the organization are not the senior executives; they are the people who actually get the job done.

Once we learn to value these people for their amazing contributions—and figure out how to convey to them our honest appreciation for those contributions—the organization can achieve greatness.

6

A Pink Cadillac in Every Garage: Motivate Others with Recognition and Celebration

ONE OF THE MOST difficult leadership tasks is *motivation*. Despite all the thinking, talking, and practicing that has gone on over the years, motivation is still an art that evades many.

What is motivation? Is it something intrinsic, something that people already have inside of them, waiting to be unlocked? Or is it something external, something that skillful leaders instill in the people they lead? Is it a word that should be used only when people are moved to achieve goals that they never thought were possible? Or can one be motivated to be mediocre?

As a manager and a student of management I have a number of observations. First, there are the occasional people, maybe one in ten, who arrive at an enterprise's doorstep fully motivated to achieve exceptional results. Equally, there are those unhappy people who are committed to mediocrity and underachievement, maybe another 10 percent of the population.

In the middle is where most people reside. We have some degree of self-respect, and we certainly want to do more than the bare minimum. But either we think we are not capable of extraordinary performance or we are not motivated to achieve it. We're the great middle: probably 80 percent of the population.

Here's the interesting thing: The success of an organization depends less on motivating that top 10 percent and far more on motivating the rest of us—we who either don't believe we're capable of excellence or are unwilling to exert the energy necessary to achieve it.

Some people might disagree, but here's my reasoning: All the organizations in the competitive arena already have the benefit of that top 10 percent's contributions. Those people are already motivated to succeed and excel. You generally cannot deter them from achieving their personal objectives or add much to the fire in their bellies. Although as a manager you never want to write off entire categories of people, working extra hard on the bottom 10 percent is probably a case of banging your head against the wall.

So that leaves us with the great middle. The level of motivation that resides in the middle 80 percent is what determines the ability of an organization to achieve sustainable performance.

By extension, motivation is *not* the ability to get people to do their jobs at the level of ability that they already think they possess. Instead, motivation is the ability to get individuals to perform at levels that exceed their self-perception or their motivation to perform. But how can a great leader get the middle 80 percent to perform?

Evidence suggests that money isn't necessarily the answer. At one corporate call center the senior managers believed that the reason they had high turnover was the nearly minimum wage levels paid at the center. An outside consultant studied the situation and concluded that in fact pay was not the problem. Management simply did not understand the importance of relationships, especially in regard to recognition.

Within six months the consultant was able to save the company $250,000 a quarter in training costs simply by reducing turnover in the call center. The secret: emphasizing recognition and relationships.

One interesting aspect of recognition is that its success depends less on the "what" than on the "how." The same reward can mean very different things in different contexts. For example, in some companies the awarding of a car or a bonus is taken for granted; it's just another "ho-hum" event. At others the same award is meaningful and motivational.

At Mary Kay sales force incentives involve much more than pink Cadillacs. In fact, the case can be made that the company does more than almost any other company when it comes to the two R's—recognition and relationships—for its sales force.

Why People Excel

What would happen to the Olympics if there were no medals, no press coverage, and no publicity surrounding the winners of each event? What would happen if the Indianapolis 500 had seating for only a few family members and there was no radio, television, or other media coverage of the race? What if winning one of these events had absolutely no larger-world significance at all?

Sure, there would be some diehards who would compete in complete isolation, out of pure love of the sport. But lots more people would decide that in light of the lack of recognition, the years of sacrifice necessary to succeed simply weren't worth it.

Recognition is one of the most powerful motivators. Money may be the way we keep score, but recognition is what puts fire in the belly. One of Mary Kay's best Independent Sales Directors explained how she motivated herself to achieve greater heights. She had read about an Olympic athlete who practiced standing in the gold-medal position as his national anthem played. For months she drew a mental picture of herself up on the Seminar stage, surrounded by her friends and colleagues, getting recognized for outstanding achievement. She picked the music that would be playing in the background (she knew that this was one of the aspects of the ceremony), and she didn't just stop at drawing a mental picture— she actually got herself a sturdy box and climbed onto it to do her visualizing.

I love to race sailboats. A few years ago I was racing a 28-foot boat at a local racing club. In that particular series I had chosen to race in the "nonspinnaker" fleet. A spinnaker is the large, colorful sail on the front of the boat that looks a little like a large balloon. The spinnaker scoops up the smallest breeze, and its use makes a boat quite a bit faster. My group of boats (without spinnakers) started five minutes behind the fleet outfitted with spinnakers.

All I was really focusing on was whether my crew of eight and I were winning against our own fleet, and we were, every time. We were doing great. I was vaguely aware of the spinnaker-equipped boats around us, and I was aware that we were beating many of them too, although we weren't even in the same race.

After the seven-race series was over, it came time to pick up our trophies. The trophies were nice, of course, but my crew and I were mainly basking in the afterglow of our winning series. It was nice to win, but I had few real emotions beyond that simple feeling. Until, that is, Charlie—one of the most senior and respected members of the club—came up to me just after the trophy ceremony.

There I was, in front of my crew and peers in the sailboat club, and Charlie addressed me. "Do you realize what you did?" he asked. "Do you realize that your boat started five minutes behind the spinnaker fleet and still finished first or second in *that* fleet? And you did that in every race! I just want you to know that the race committee boat watched you the entire series, and we are really impressed by your crew's phenomenal work."

Yes, I enjoyed winning those races, but I sail mainly because I love it. (I'm one of those people who would sail alone in the dark in the rain, if necessary.) I rarely get excited about a win from a personal standpoint because 90 percent of winning a sailboat race has to do with the crew—the team—rather than the skipper. But I must admit that when Charlie walked up in front of all those people and declared a "job well done," it made me feel *great*.

Recognition—the right recognition—is one of the most powerful motivators there is. It is why ice skaters get up at five in the morning for years to practice. It is why they (and their families) spend hundreds of thousands of dollars and dedicate years of their lives to the pursuit of a dream. They see themselves stepping up on that podium and hearing their country's national anthem played. It is the picture of a dream. That moment of ultimate recognition drives people to achieve great things in their lives.

Recognition Makes the World Go Round

If you ask people about their most memorable moments on the job, their answers are often surprising. They don't often tell you about the specifics of the big deal they closed or the promotion they got. Far more often they tell you about what someone said to them about their accomplishment. They tell you about the ceremony that surrounded the event.

One of the things that is interesting about the Mary Kay Inc. sales force is that money rarely is mentioned. Certainly the fact that some of these women make six-figure incomes each year is important, and yes, money is discussed on occasion. But what is more important to these people, almost across the board, is (1) the accomplishment and (2) the *recognition* of that accomplishment.

What is going on here? Many of the most successful women in this group would never have had any kind of career had it not been for Mary Kay Inc. Add to that the fact that this opportunity attracts women from every stratum—from the highly educated, to the immigrant, to the housewife who's never worked outside the home—including some who weren't supposed to accomplish anything.

Women like Independent National Sales Director Wanda Dalby, for example.

Dalby grew up the last child in a family of nine children. As the youngest in her family, she had always been looked upon as the most immature. She was teased mercilessly about her looks, her hair, her shyness, and so on. But as she grew older, things turned around for her. Eventually she married a dentist and from all outward appearances "had it all."

After a number of years of a marriage in which she wasn't expected to work at all, Dalby decided that she wanted to do something for herself. She was still extremely shy, and she still lacked confidence and self-esteem. When her brothers and sisters found out that she had decided to set up a business selling Mary Kay products, they were not particularly supportive. In fact, they were so sure she was going to fail that they laughed out loud at her.

Her husband was even less encouraging. He used her momentous decision as an opportunity to assert that she had no abilities that would lend themselves to being a good marketer—or anything else, for that matter. He made it clear that he thought it was absolutely ridiculous that she would consider entering the direct-sales business.

Despite being written off by her husband and family, Dalby became relentless in her pursuit of excellence and succeeded magnificently. Several years into her highly successful career she was asked to give a speech at a meeting in Dallas. Like so many of her colleagues, when faced with this juncture, she was paralyzed with fear. But a Mary Kay staff member sent a message from Mary Kay herself. "You need to do this," the message said in so many words. "You've succeeded, and you have an obligation to share your story. It is really important that you help others understand what it took for you to excel."

Dalby understood and made the speech. The unspoken point? Even a young woman working against enormous odds can succeed—and get recognized for that success. Hundreds, perhaps thousands, of women in the audience got the message and resolved to earn similar recognition for themselves.

Celebrating Wins

The title of this book, *More Than a Pink Cadillac*, was chosen in part with the theme of recognition in mind. Can you imagine what it means to women like Wanda Dalby when they go beyond the bounds of what anybody ever expected of them—indeed, what they expected of themselves—and step up on the stage to receive their first pink Cadillac?

Do you think they ever consider the dollar value of the award? Of course not. The dollar value of that car is the farthest thing from their minds. What they are holding in their minds is their *accomplishment*, which now is being recognized in such a conspicuous way. They are holding in their minds the picture of just how far they've come.

Another Independent National Sales Director, Darlene Berggren, well remembers the ribbing she took from her colleagues and her boss at the corporate headquarters of the major airline where she had worked when she first started selling Mary Kay products. The day she earned the use of her pink Cadillac, Berggren drove to the headquarters and parked the car in her former boss's parking spot, right outside his office window.

"When he saw the pink Cadillac," she recalls, "he invited me into his office and apologized, saying how sorry he was he had discouraged me so."

Yet another Independent National Sales Director, Nancy Tietjen— who had worked the graveyard shift loading shotgun shells before establishing a Mary Kay business—picked up her first pink Cadillac and headed straight for her local gas station. Again and again she drove back and forth over the hose that rang the bell inside. She wanted to drive home a point to the attendants inside, the same guys who had laughed at her and scoffed at her dreams as they had put a dollar's worth of gas in her dilapidated old car. Now no more rotten floorboards and no more derision.

For a woman who was one of the original five Cadillac drivers in 1969 when the pink Cadillac program began, this fine car was the very first car she ever owned. National Sales Director Emeritus Lovie Quinn had built her business by borrowing a ride and taking a bus because her husband needed the family's only car for his business. Still another Independent National Sales Director Emeritus, Ila Burgardt, had grown up in poverty and raised two children as a single mother. The first year that both she and her sister earned the use of pink Cadillacs, they returned triumphantly to the small Oklahoma town of their youth and proudly paraded up and down Main Street, honking and waving from their shiny new cars. The local newspaper covered the ad hoc parade and the accomplishments that had made it possible.

For most of these women the pink Cadillac represents a victory of will over doubt. It is a victory of effort and determination over discouragement.

How many people ever get to realize their potential? Conversely, how many organizations are filled to the brim with talented people who are spending their lives doing less than their best? With the answers to those questions in mind, think about the absolutely powerful moment of recognition, that moment when your peers get to see the results of years of perseverance and sacrifice coming to fruition, all in one wonderful moment.

That's what recognition and celebration can create in an organization. Recognition and celebration are the keys to encouraging people to discover talents that they never knew existed. Companies that achieve greatness are those which help others achieve their potential by making a really big deal out of each significant accomplishment. Mary Kay used to tell the members of her successful sales force that they had defied the odds. She would say, "Many women go to their graves with their music left unplayed." Thousands of successful Mary Kay Independent Beauty Consultants, Independent Sales Directors, and Independent National Sales Directors have used the company to "play their music" and realize their dreams.

Tom Whatley, president of global sales and marketing, offers the following observations on the power of recognition:

> *Most organizations work within the classic "80/20" standard; that is, 20 percent of the people are responsible for 80 percent of the organization's success. But not all organizations have the tools to move those in the 80 percent group into the 20 percent group. In the sales group—that's where my teams spend a good bit of their time—we like to see ordinary women set and attain extraordinary goals. We practice the art of "praising people to success." In the Mary Kay world it is recognition that causes ordinary people to rise to extraordinary performance.*
>
> *Mary Kay would say that attitude determines altitude. And to this phrase she'd almost always add the most famous encouraging words, "You can do it!" And I've seen firsthand the power of that phrase. I attended a luncheon at our Career Conference in Detroit, where I was seated next to an Independent Beauty Consultant who told me that her ultimate goal was to earn the use of a pink Cadillac. I remembered that I had picked up some Cadillac lapel pins from the General Motors headquarters, which I had visited the morning of this luncheon. I reached into my pocket and handed the woman one of those lapel pins.*
>
> *"You will turn this pin into a Cadillac," I told her. "You can do it." Well, a year later the same woman approached me at another meeting. She had earned her Cadillac!*
>
> *So now we include this pin in the letter I send to all of our*

sales directors who are on target for a Cadillac. And when the brand-new Independent Sales Directors come to Dallas for education sessions, we make sure there's a pink Cadillac parked outside. On a tour of our corporate offices I greet these new sales directors and offer them the chance to have their photo taken with me holding a poster of the new Cadillac. It works.

My point is that recognition is not a onetime event. It is a constant in the course of motivating an individual into the 20 percent group . . . one step at a time. Also constant is the way in which recognition is handled. The sincerity, the medium, and the way in which it is designed to trigger that next step . . . the achievement of higher goals.

Seminar: Stand Up and Be Recognized!

Every summer, as was noted in an earlier chapter, Mary Kay Inc. takes over the Dallas Convention Center for about a month. During that month the company holds five successive events called Seminar for the purpose of recognizing the accomplishments of its independent sales force and revealing new programs, plans, and products. By the month's end almost 50,000 Mary Kay Independent Beauty Consultants will have attended Seminar.

Like any convention, it provides an opportunity to be educated, networked, and be introduced to new products. But there is much more than that to a Mary Kay Seminar. The company spares no expense, making every effort to reach out to each and every independent sales force participant in a way that is meaningful and motivating.

For many people Seminar attendance is a time when they first become bonded to the Mary Kay way and its culture. It is for all the ultimate delivery on the promise that Mary Kay made in her marketing plan: "You are in business *for* yourself but not *by* yourself."

She loved reminding these women—independent contractors— that they are presidents of their own companies. This concept makes Mary Kay Inc. significantly different from most other companies and, once understood, puts Seminar in perspective.

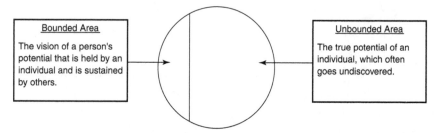

FIGURE 6–1. Recognition and encouragement.

Assume that Figure 6–1 represents two aspects of a person. The small circular area represents both a person's accomplishments and what that person thinks she or he can do. The larger area represents the area in which the individual has abilities but does not think she or he is capable of performing. In most businesses an individual is expected to remain within the limited area in which he or she has a history of performance and in which that individual thinks he or she can perform. That's it. I call that a bounded image. In each of us, however, there is an unbounded area. That is the area in which we have skills and potential to do significantly more than we or the people around us believe possible.

Better than perhaps any other figure in contemporary business, Mary Kay Ash understood that the unbounded area is a place most women will never go, at least without strong encouragement. At the same time, she believed strongly in the abilities of women. She said if they had desire and a willingness to work hard, there literally were no bounds.

Helping Others Exceed Expectations

At Mary Kay, independent sales force members are encouraged to break boundaries. Even in their moments of triumph they are encouraged to get out of their comfort zones. There are stories aplenty about an Independent Sales Director walking across the stage to accept accolades for having raised the bar on her accomplishments. Mary Kay would stand at center stage and hug and congratulate her on, say, her achievement of

$1 million in unit sales. Then she would lean close and whisper, "Try for $1.2 million next year!"

Indeed, many a story has been told of a woman beating her best simply on the grounds that she had promised Mary Kay she would. Instead of focusing on the bounded area of the individual, in other words, this organization and its leaders go out of their way to help the members of the independent sales force go beyond the bounds to discover their potential. Mary Kay described such women as being like rosebuds: "all closed up." It was her greatest joy, she often said, to watch them blossom before her eyes.

When and if they need it, the Mary Kay organization is there to help them go over the next hurdle. Independent National Sales Director Lisa Madson, for example, was struggling to best a sales force record unit annual sales figure of $2 million. The deadline was close, and she was beginning to doubt her ability to break that particular record. In the mail from the staff in Dallas came a box full of broken records with a message enclosed: "Records are made to be broken."

The next week's mail brought a box of 20 candy bars—the $100 Grand brand—to remind her she could eat this $2 million elephant one bite at a time.

These small incentives serve as a reminder to every Mary Kay independent sales force member that she has an entire company cheering her on and wishing her well in her effort to attain a lofty goal.

At Mary Kay recognition and motivation can give wings to some pretty amazing dreams. They also can put braces on teeth, pay college tuition, and permit husbands to take early retirement or pursue their own business dreams.

A Coronation of Impossible Achievement

One way to get a glimpse of what Seminar really means is to take a look at the lives of a few recent attendees. All three of the following stories were featured at the Seminar in 2001, when the company focused on "enriching women's lives." The three women featured were not among the highest achievers in terms of sales figures, but their stories emphasized the importance of motivation and encouragement. What is important to understand, though, is that almost everyone in the Mary Kay independent sales force has a similar story. It is the story of doing what they thought was not possible.

Story 1.   Amber was an 18-year-old college student who discovered Mary Kay Inc. during her first year in college. Amber was able to blend her sales activities with her studies in order to supplement her college expenses. It wasn't long before she told her parents that she would be able to pay for her own college expenses completely. Now out of college, Amber talked about her dream of working hard to purchase ranch land for her horses.

One of the things that made Amber successful was what she termed "setting goals that scared me." It was very clear that the support and encouragement of her Mary Kay family provided the impetus for her success and would continue to do so. Incidentally, Amber's mom—inspired by her daughter's success—also began a Mary Kay business.

Story 2.   Bonnie, a single parent, saw the Mary Kay opportunity as a way to provide for her family. Bonnie was six and a half weeks from qualifying for the use of a Mary Kay career car when her 15-year-old Buick with 185,000 miles on it gave out on her. For most people that would have been the end of the story, but not for Bonnie. Her Independent Mary Kay Sales Director, three of her fellow Independent Beauty Consultants, and even one customer came to the rescue. They encouraged her not to give up on her dreams. More important, they lent her their own cars for the next six weeks so that she could get her daughter to school and continue working. Of course, Bonnie qualified for the career car.

Story 3.   Michelle was a divorced mother of four young children who had a part-time Mary Kay business to earn spending money. One day, as she was sitting at home caring for her infant, the phone rang. The message was chilling: "Your ex-husband has had a mental breakdown and has decided that he wants to kill you and the children. Get out of the house immediately, do not take time to pack anything, get your children out of school, and get out of the state."

Frantically, Michelle rushed to follow the instructions she was given. She ended up at the train station with nothing but her four children, the clothes on her back, and a cooler to hold infant formula and snacks for the children. They fled to a women's shelter in another state.

During that harrowing ordeal her Mary Kay Independent Sales Director, a close friend, gave Michelle the encouragement she needed to carry on in the face of this devastating personal tragedy. Although Michelle had literally nothing to her name, she was expecting a refund from her previous year's tax return. When the refund came in, she used it to buy inventory and get a voice mail pager so that she could restart her Mary Kay business. Michelle was able to get short-term child care for her children so that she could keep her selling appointments. Since she had no car, she had to take a taxi to get to those appointments. If she made a sale, she had to take the taxi to the bank to deposit the money so that she could continue to buy more inventory.

It wasn't long before Michelle sold her way out of poverty and was again able to provide for her children. Michelle credits the Mary Kay world with helping her achieve her goals. "You never know what this can do for you," says Michelle, who eventually earned the use of a pink Cadillac and bought a home.

At Seminar, as women receive the prizes of their choosing—be it a trip, a piece of jewelry, or furniture for an office suite—they are making good on the dreams of the firm's founder. The faces change, along with the details of the inspiring stories, but the *instilling of belief* remains a constant. As they receive their prizes, most comment that someone came along to motivate them to go beyond what they thought they could do. They recognize those who reached out to make a difference, the ones who've been around to celebrate each success along the way and ultimately coach them to do things they never thought they were capable of achieving.

Without fail, they promise they'll be back the next year and the next. The pattern for success has been set in their lives. They do not expect mediocrity; they expect to go beyond what they ever thought they could do.

They also have learned the Mary Kay practice of encouraging other people to succeed. Invariably, at her moment of triumph, one of these successful women will point high up in the rafters of the cavernous Dallas Convention Center. She'll call out the obscure row in the second balcony where she sat the first time she came to Seminar. She will tell the woman in that seat—and all those anywhere near her—that "you can do it." The room erupts in cheers. One more woman has discovered how great she really is, and she is eager to take others in the room along with her on the journey.

Moving the Hearts and Minds of Others: Motivation

It all comes down to motivation, and the heart of motivation is recognition and encouragement.

Mary Kay Ash was a master of motivation. In the early days, when a new Independent Beauty Consultant would have a horrible week and sell only $100 of products, instead of being discouraged, Mary Kay would celebrate the accomplishment. She would use that small success to encourage the consultant to set a higher goal. She would remind the woman that she could achieve anything she committed herself to achieving.

Recognition/Encouragement

Each Seminar year brings a new crop of women who have broken their own "belief barriers," and the process of encouraging, motivating, and recognizing begins anew. At the end of each Seminar the slate is wiped clean. The playing field is evened once again. Everyone starts over building on the next year's accomplishments and the next year's dreams.

Anyone is welcome to throw her hat into the ring of recognition and honor because, as Mary Kay planned it, there is room at the top for everyone who cares to go there. There is a career ladder to climb in order to get there. After experiencing Seminar, even the woman in the last row of the top balcony is picturing herself achieving great things. The seed has been planted. She believes that a higher goal can be achieved. If she takes home that tiny piece of belief and nothing more, Seminar has been a success.

The Unbelievable Power of Recognition

The difference between a mediocre organization and a great one is its people, yet most companies start the game with a similar group of people. At the end of the game, though, the company whose leadership recognizes and expects excellence outperforms the other company. Why? Because inside each person there is a desire to accomplish great things. More often than not people achieve those great goals when they have a leader who believes in them and praises them to excellence.

7

The Heritage Department:
Never Leave Your Values

ONE OF THE stubborn realities of organizations is that they deteriorate. If you look at the most successful companies of the last century, only a handful—literally—have been able to sustain their original success on a long-term basis.

The reasons are many and complex. Markets change, leadership places a big bet in the wrong direction, or new technology disrupts or even wipes out an industry.

Or—and this is surprisingly common—the organization's leaders fail to remember what got them to the top in the first place.

In Chapter 4 we looked at the problem inherent in focusing an organization on its historical competencies: An obsession with honing yesterday's skills is not likely to be productive in the long run. Now I'm going to make a second assertion that may seem to contradict the first one: Organizations that forget their traditions are likely to get into deep trouble.

How do these two statements fit together? The answer is fairly straightforward. A company's leadership needs to be prepared to forget about *what* the firm has always done well and at the same time remember *how* it has done those things well. The "how" I'm thinking about involves the company's *values*.

If the company has done well, that success probably is due in large part to its values. If the company is to continue to thrive, it has to understand and nourish those values. Sometimes people associate values with rigidity or inflexibility. I think the opposite is true. When corporate values are allowed to deteriorate, a firm gets less flexible. It gets less adept at both responding to market changes and anticipating future customer needs. The key is to focus on the practices and principles that created the company in the first place. Values allow a company's leadership to discover what the company must become, grounded in the good things it has been.

Mary Kay Ash understood this paradox. I suspect that this is one reason she was so consistent—even adamant—about sustaining the values of her company. One of the values that she worked hardest to foster was an entrepreneurial outlook. The problem with many successful companies, as we've seen, is complacency. (Mary Kay Ash warned about such companies, saying that "a laurel sat upon wilts.") These companies begin as creative, risk-taking, and entrepreneurial ventures and wind up as slow-moving dinosaurs.

Of course, many scholars and managers have remarked on the phenomenon by which a vital company slowly ossifies. Professor Howard Stevenson of the Harvard Business School, for example, talks about the gradual shift from being *opportunity-driven* to being *resource-driven*. It's certainly an understandable drift: As you get successful, you have resources—money, for example—that you never had back in the scrappy entrepreneurial days. You have something valuable to protect, and so you get conservative.

Consider Figure 7–1, which reflects the findings of a number of studies that have been done on organizations.

Note the two key trends captured in these graphs. First, as companies age, the level of entrepreneurial behavior (including creativity and risk taking) slowly declines. Meanwhile, a more or less massive corporate bureaucracy is entrenching itself. As the organization loses its ability to introduce new products, invade new markets, and pursue new

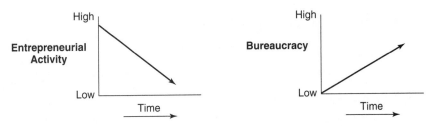

FIGURE 7-1. Relationship between levels of entrepreneurial activity and bureaucracy.

opportunities, the cost center grows slowly but surely in terms of size and influence.

At some point, inevitably, the "ox is in the ditch." The bureaucracy-driven (and "resource-driven") senior management team is unable to solve the problem or perhaps even to identify it. As I have pointed out in a number of my writings, when companies get into trouble this deep, they tend to start chasing the latest management fad in hopes that it will fix the problem. It won't, because fad solutions can do little more than address symptoms rather than the problem itself.

Once again, the real problem is that they've forgotten who brought them to the ball in the first place. They have stuck with the "what" and lost sight of the "how." They are unwilling to move out of their traditional comfort zone—yesterday's products and practices—and embrace a changing market.

Many corporate executives pay lip service to corporate culture. The companies they lead have mission statements, and their Web sites have areas called "our tradition of service" or some other soothing thing. But many of these organizations fail to act as if they believed that powerful links exist between the corporate culture, the values that drive that culture, and corporate performance. This is puzzling because studies of Fortune 500 companies as well as companies around the world show clearly that inappropriate cultures (and values) can hurt profitability to a startling degree.

I say that the converse has to be true: Appropriate cultures and their associated values can propel a company to greatness.

Learning to Sustain Values

If you take the time to peruse one or more of Mary Kay Ash's three books, you will discover that she clearly understood the impact of culture and values on the bottom line. One could even argue that she made it the central theme of her life's work. Even though those books were written between one and two decades ago, many of the ideas contained in them retain their freshness. This explains in part why today's leaders at Mary Kay Inc. find it relatively easy to get direction and set a course that is compatible with the goals of the founder.

Most companies use a financial tool called variance analysis to stay on track. Variance analysis is simply a way of comparing a company's financial performance with its goals. For example, if a company budgeted for a 20 percent increase in sales over a specific time period and the actual increase was only 3 percent, that would set off alarm bells. The bigger the negative variance, of course, the louder the alarm bells.

But like so many of the tools that are available to executives, variance analyses measure the effect rather than the cause. There aren't any easy-to-wield tools that measure corporate culture and values, which I would argue are the cause of corporate success and associated profits.

Sustain the Soul

I've already mentioned the deterioration of the common bond within Mary Kay Inc. in the second half of the 1990s. That decline was the result of a gradual departure from Mary Kay Ash's personal values, which she had imprinted on the company. To their credit, once the problem was diagnosed, it wasn't long before people ranging from the senior leadership to the independent sales force made a concerted effort to lead the company back to its founding values. As an outgrowth of those efforts, the cornerstone of the company strategy beginning in 2000 was that of *sustaining the soul*.

So what's a soul, and how is it sustained?

A soul is defined as the "internal substance or being" of an individual. That internal substance is that which makes up what an individual is and therefore has a direct impact on the individual's behavior.

In assessing the company's challenges at the start of the twenty-first century and looking forward, the senior executive team decided that the very soul of the company was at stake. In other words, an erosion of values and behavioral standards was posing a threat to the well-being of the company. In a number of ways, the independent sales force leadership was making the same point.

That was when the corporate strategy was amended to include sustaining the soul as a cornerstone. That term included two important ideas:

- The company would return to the core values and principles that were articulated by Mary Kay Ash.
- The company's leadership would accept the responsibility for sustaining those founding values and principles as its long-term responsibility.

It is somewhat risky for a company to announce publicly that a major component of its corporate strategy is sustaining the soul. Lip service isn't going to be enough to meet that goal and in fact may actually work against it. (People don't want to be misled, especially in realms as important as this.) You can't simply tell a few good stories and hope that will cover it. You actually have to *live* it.

Fortunately, one person who has the ability to see how all the different pieces of the organization fit together and really "live" is Richard Rogers, the company's chairman, who is Mary Kay's son. He often is recognized for his financial expertise in guiding the company over the years since its founding. But as is often the case with Mary Kay Inc., there is more to the story. According to Brad Glendening, "Richard Rogers always understood the softer side of the business. He always knew that his mother's values, principles, and practices were the 'support system' for the company's historical success. He also realized that this would be the key to the company's future success." Despite all the other things he had on his plate when he returned as chief executive officer in 2001, Rogers immediately subscribed to the notion that "keeping the culture" was critical to the company's momentum.

Behind some of this reasoning, of course, lay the fact that after Mary Kay's death in late 2001, for the first time, the thousands of new recruits who would be signing up as members of the independent sales force would have no direct contact with the founder. Part of the challenge therefore lay in conveying in simple terms and in multiple ways exactly what the driving principles behind Mary Kay Ash had always been.

The company maintains a museum in the lobby of the corporate headquarters building. That museum relates the history of the company, and of course special attention is paid to the founder. But the museum also celebrates other contributors who embody the company's values. A new wing highlighting the Independent National Sales Directors, for example, was dedicated in 2002. It's called the Keepers of the Dream Hall of Honor.

Meanwhile, Mary Kay Inc. makes a concerted effort to ensure that the Mary Kay values are conveyed in every aspect of the company's work. The creative and field communications groups pay close attention to the details of conveying elements of "soul" in their printed, Web, and video work. There's a Culture Committee among employees—discussed at length below—a Helping Women team that works in the civic and charitable arena, and a Sales Group Pulse team that keeps its ear to the feelings of the independent sales force. There are extensive orientation sessions for the employees of Mary Kay's international subsidiaries, who travel to Dallas to understand the how and why of this unusual company.

Even the technology teams get involved. During a ramp-up for a new technology initiative, for example, all the "techie" new hires were given special training in the culture and heritage of the company. This was dubbed a "warm fuzzy" session by the technologists, who seemed to welcome a break from their high-tech routines.

New-employee orientation also involves an intensive learning experience focused on history and heritage. The senior leadership believes that every person who comes onboard must understand the company's philosophy and its focus on sustaining the soul. In a sense, this is in the spirit of full disclosure. These values are extremely important to the company; therefore, new hires should get a very clear picture of them as soon as possible.

Equally important is the way these values play out in the company's relationships with its customers. There is a focused desire to make sure that every customer is treated with the same respect that people inside the company are afforded. This is the "right" thing to do, and it's also smart business. In other words, living the heritage of the firm is the best way to live and the best way to stay competitive.

In this way, a legacy defines the future.

A "Department to Remember"

Think back to the charts in Figure 7–1 that depicted how the typical successful company faces the death of entrepreneurship and a creeping takeover by bureaucracy over the years. Now imagine what would happen if a successful company could turn those charts around, in other words, make bureaucracy go down and creativity go up as the years go by. Such a company, built on a strong foundation, would be virtually unstoppable.

Now think about the structure of Mary Kay Inc., which is literally a company of entrepreneurs. Every year new entrepreneurs join the independent sales force, with high expectations of success. Many start with next to nothing and are determined to make their mark. This attitude, along with this regular infusion of new talent, is one of the great drivers of the company.

To state it the other way around, the demise of the entrepreneurial spirit at any company is troublesome; in a company like Mary Kay it could be disastrous. That's why early in the year 2000 the organization took another step to ensure that the rich history and the values of the company would be sustained by setting up something called the Corporate Heritage Department.

Corporate Heritage is charged with distilling and disseminating the colorful history of the company. It continues the ongoing efforts to understand and celebrate the contributions of the founder and also interprets the current evolution of the company in terms of values and heritage.

This is motivated partly by a desire to differentiate the company from its competitors. "If you build a uniqueness that is hard to copy," says Tom Whatley, president of global sales and marketing, "it provides yet another leg up on the competition. And in fact, we are doing things here that many companies only dream of."

It's not just a question of image making. It's about genuine actions, which make the difference over the long run. Living your values through authentic actions is a key lifeline for the company's 900,000 independent sales entrepreneurs. "A lot of people do not understand that this company exists to support a lot of businesses around the world," Whatley explains. "We recognize that 900,000 independent businesswomen around the world are counting on us to maintain our values in order to support their success."

Of course, other companies are committed to understanding and invoking their heritage. The furniture maker Herman Miller celebrates what it calls "tribal storytellers." The apparel maker Nike allows members of its senior executive ranks to add "corporate storyteller" to their titles if they qualify. In the Corporate Heritage Department at Mary Kay Inc. that person is Yvonne Pendleton. Pendleton, an award-winning journalist and former newspaper editor, is the writer who worked most closely with Mary Kay Ash throughout the 1990s. On the basis of that experience, she says, she believes one of the strongest assets Mary Kay Inc. has brought into the twenty-first century is the wisdom and sayings of its founder. Visiting the Mary Kay headquarters or attending an event for the independent sales force confirms Pendleton's observation: Almost everywhere you go, you will hear Mary Kay Ash quoted. "The wisdom of the founder's messages of caring and concern is woven through the very fiber of this company," says Pendleton.

But it's not only the "people people" or the "people functions" that worry about spreading the Mary Kay Ash system of beliefs. President and Chief Operating Officer (COO) David Holl, perhaps the executive who worries the most about quantitative issues, is unlikely to plunge into a sophisticated monologue about earnings before depreciation, interest, taxes, and amortization (EBDITA) or other critical measures without first invoking words such as *belief* and *heart*.

As one might expect, however, the place where the wisdom and values of Mary Kay Ash are inscribed most indelibly is in the hearts of the giant independent sales force. Here, it seems, the enduring legacy of the company's founder shines most brightly, perhaps because these are the very people who have benefited the most from her determination to change women's lives for the better.

Their level of commitment is no accident. These people lived the dream, and they also had the dream explained to them many times over and in many contexts. Especially with the independent sales force, Mary Kay always took the time to explain her principles and the important role they would play, not only in the success of her company but also in the lives of the women she touched. She explained it, told stories to illustrate it, published books and columns on it, and asked leaders at corporate headquarters and in the sales force to pick up whenever she left off. And she did that over and over again so that everyone would benefit from this learning.

"As a result," says Pendleton, "we became very aware of the importance of our culture. I would say we are as proficient at teaching the values as we are at recognition and praise." Among Pendleton's most valued possessions are three-inch-thick notebooks bulging with real-life stories. "People relate to stories," says Pendleton. "Mary Kay had a story for every situation. We take our cues from her.

"If, for instance, she wanted to drive home the point that everyone can make a difference in this world, she would tell a story to illustrate that. If she needed to illustrate that there is greatness inside each person, she would tell another story. And there were always new stories because Mary Kay was always listening carefully. She could find a message, a learning point, in most of what she read and heard."

Mary Kay Ash particularly liked relating stories about members of the independent sales force. "She called me one day," Pendleton recalls, "to tell me she'd just met a pediatrician who'd given up medicine for a Mary Kay business. 'What do you think this means?' she asked me. So I thought I'd better find out."

Pendleton called the pediatrician: "You can imagine Mary Kay's delight when she learned that this doctor had discovered that she could affect more lives and help more children by helping their mothers through her Mary Kay business. And of course Mary Kay loved hearing that the doctor was keeping in touch with medicine by volunteering at a free children's clinic in her city."

Mary Kay Ash often would use a real-life story to illustrate what a skilled mother does when, for example, her child is diagnosed with a learning disability or she faces other unforeseen demands of motherhood. Also, there were many stories that recognize the journey of overcoming low self-esteem: "Mary Kay would relate a story about a now-successful Independent Sales Director who in a previous occupation had gone to work in a feed store, where she been given a used smock with someone else's name stitched on it to wear on the job. She would use this example to inspire women to celebrate being their own bosses, and to take pride in their work.

"Mary Kay passed on to us a highly developed sense of emotional intelligence about how a company should be led and how its people should be treated," Pendleton explains. "She also left us a set of timeless founding principles that apply just as well today as they did in 1963. We intend to keep talking about—keep *living*—those principles so that they remain integral in all of our lives. This is much like the baton in a relay race: We keep handing it on to the next person and the next. And that's the most exciting part about what we've inherited: It's a timeless treasure that can continue to be handed down."

Mary Kay's core values have been part of the company's teaching for many years. The values and mission statement below are featured in company literature, on tapes, and on the Web site:

Core Values

- *Integrity*—Integrity and the Golden Rule must guide every business decision.
- *Enthusiasm*—Enthusiasm encourages a positive attitude and provides inspiration as we work together to achieve our goals.
- *Praise*—Praise motivates everyone to reach their full potential.
- *Leadership*—Leadership among our sales force and employees must be encouraged and recognized in order to achieve long-term success.

- *Quality*—Quality in our products and services must be a priority in order for us to deliver value and satisfaction to our customers.
- *Teamwork*—Teamwork allows each person to be valued and appreciated by others while contributing to the Company's success.
- *Service*—Service should be prompt and proactive to provide convenience with a personal touch.
- *Balance*—Balance in our lives with God, family, and career in harmony.

Mission Statement

Mary Kay's mission is to enrich women's lives.

We will do this in tangible ways, by offering quality products to consumers, financial opportunities to our independent sales force, and fulfilling careers to our employees.

We also will reach out to the hearts and spirits of women by enabling personal growth and fulfillment for the women whose lives we touch.

We will carry out our mission in a spirit of caring, living the positive values on which our company was built.

A Paycheck of the Heart

According to the corporate counsel, Brad Glendening, Mary Kay Ash had a favorite phrase she used whenever she wanted to compliment someone. "Thank you," she would say. "You've given me a paycheck of the heart."

It is no coincidence that the first hardcover book published by the company that was not written by Mary Kay Ash is on the subject of living the principles of Mary Kay Ash. It's titled *Paychecks of the Heart*, and it consists of stories told by the Independent National Sales Directors.

"These women are the torchbearers for the Mary Kay way," says Glendening. "They're the first generation of sales force leaders, and it is to them that Mary Kay assigned the care and nurturing of the independent sales force. They are the ones who carry forth the values that Mary Kay role modeled for her sales force leaders."

Glendening points to three specific changes that Mary Kay Ash and her company helped bring about in the U.S. workplace, all of which created opportunities for women:

- Flextime. "When women praise flextime, they should realize that they owe a lot to Mary Kay Ash. Flextime was unheard of in the business world of the mid-1960s. The marketing plan she created has allowed so many women to contribute to the well-being of their families and also participate in the economy."
- Cracking the glass ceiling. "When women declare victory over glass ceilings, they are in part applauding the efforts of Mary Kay, who knew that women could soar if someone would give them an opportunity and a track to run on. She was operating on this principle 20 years before that phrase was coined."
- Balanced priorities. "When women maintain their femininity, their motherhood, and their family roles and still become successful business owners, they are living out the dream of Mary Kay, who since 1963 preached balance and priorities as a way for women to have it all."

One goal in all the storytelling that goes on at Mary Kay Inc. is to help people learn from their failures as well as from their victories. People generally learn more from defeats than from victories, assuming, of course, that their context allows for this kind of learning, which Mary Kay referred to as "failing forward to success." Learning is a positive experience; therefore, learning from mistakes (understandably viewed as negatives) is by definition a positive experience.

Glendening speaks to the issue of storytelling at Mary Kay Inc.:

Mary Kay Ash coined a phrase for the telling of a story with the intent to inspire or motivate others. It's called the I-story. Our independent sales force leaders and even our employees are encouraged to share their I-stories.

In addition to inspiring others, these stories express the heartfelt gratitude we have for Mary Kay and her life-changing values. Telling your I-story is also a way to connect to the heart and show gratitude. You'll hear stories of great triumphs over obstacles and about gaining self-esteem or overcoming shyness.

There is always gratitude for the difference Mary Kay has made in someone's life. There is great strength in connecting like this. As Mary Kay used to say, "We never know whose story or what circumstance might inspire yet another woman."

The content of dreams changes over the years. To generalize greatly, women's dreams have gotten larger over the past 40 years. For example, one of the first two Independent National Sales Directors, now Emeritus Helen McVoy, loved to recount in her I-story that she first pursued her Mary Kay career for no other reason than to buy ivy for her garden room. Nearly 40 years later, by contrast, another up-and-coming Independent Sales Director—one who had financed her college education with a Mary Kay business—told of her dream: to buy ranch land for her horses near the Hearst Castle in California.

Thus, in the process of gaining economic clout and independence, women also have learned to set their sights higher. But although the dreams related in I-stories may have grown larger, the dreaming remains the same. The universal truth Mary Kay learned very early is that every woman looks to find a better life for herself and her family.

"I give Mary Kay Ash great credit," says Glendening. "She not only figured out what makes women tick as far as recognition and motivation, she created the network, the support, and the encouragement that would allow them to thrive.

"And these aren't just American success stories. The stories are equally compelling all over the world. For example, Mary Kay Ash enjoyed relating the story of what happened when she attended a company event in Germany shortly after the fall of the Berlin Wall. A woman from East Germany who was a new Independent Beauty Consultant came across the stage to meet Mary Kay. She took Mary Kay's hand and then grabbed the microphone and excitedly said, 'First we have freedom, and now we have Mary Kay!' "

No matter what the language, there's an interesting two-part sentence that women around the world have used to describe the transformational aspect of their relationship with Mary Kay Inc. "I got into a Mary Kay business to earn extra money," they say in so many words, "and it wasn't long before Mary Kay got into *me*."

Sustaining the Soul with the Culture Committee

I've already mentioned the Culture Committee. Years ago Mary Kay Ash stated what has become the core challenge of the Culture Committee: "When we were a small company, we worked very hard at becoming a large company. Now that we are a large company, we work very hard at keeping the atmosphere of a small company."

I have observed this company both in its "small days" and in its current sprawling form, and I'm comfortable saying that the Culture Committee (and related corporate mechanisms) has done its part. Even though the company is not located in that small building in West Dallas anymore, and even though it operates in 30 markets around the world, the enthusiasm and attitude are the same today as they were back then.

The Culture Committee focuses on the corporate organization rather than the independent sales organization. Its stated purpose is to "preserve the culture of the organization by supporting Mary Kay's Mission, enabling a positive work environment where employees find fulfilling careers, personal growth, and the opportunity to enrich others' lives."

A lot of organizations operate on the premise that turnover is good. Among other things, turnover allows an organization to keep salaries down by replacing older, more expensive employees with new, lower-paid employees. At Mary Kay Inc., by contrast, senior managers are interested in making sure that people do *not* leave.

Senior executives also listen carefully to input from the various "pulse" groups, which keep a sharp ear attuned to issues in the field and inside the corporation. Every employee in the firm is encouraged to communicate with these committees for the purpose of enhancing the work experience at Mary Kay Inc.

An example of the work done by one such a committee is the creation of the "Ten Leadership Practice Rules," which are taught and used throughout the company. As the daily participation of Mary Kay Ash in the life of the company declined, this committee felt that it was important to make sure that her leadership practices were identified and sustained. As a result, the 10 rules are a standard across the company today. (These rules will be discussed at length in a later chapter.)

One way that the pulse approach is kept fresh and innovative is by making sure that the committees always have a blend of seasoned employees and newer employees. This blending of the "Mary Kay experience" often provides new insights into ways to focus on sustaining the company's historical values.

Humble Perseverance

Is all this effort paying off?

Once again, there are no easy cause-and-effect lessons to be learned. It's impossible to prove that the company's long record of consistent double-digit annual growth is the result of its investments in its heritage. It's impossible to prove that the company's successful push into the global economy derives from its traditions.

But the anecdotal evidence in support of such claims is voluminous. Mary Kay Inc. receives thousands of letters each month from people whose lives have been touched by the company and those who try to practice Mary Kay Ash's values in their own lives. These letters come from Sales Directors, their families, and others who have been affected positively.

There's some kind of "formula" at work, and it works very well. Perhaps one would expect the "owners" of that formula—the people who run the company that markets "America's Best Selling Brand" of facial skin care and color cosmetics[1]—to be cocky or even arrogant. In my experience, this isn't the case. Competitors aren't derided; in fact, their strengths are well known, lauded, and in some cases imitated. There is an attitude of what might be described as humble perseverance.

No, these aren't words that you will ever hear around the company. But I believe that if you study Mary Kay Inc. carefully, you will see an organization that is determined to keep learning and keep getting better. This, by definition, demands a certain humility. (If I still have things to learn, I'm far from perfect.) It is also an organization that is determined to keep growing and keep providing new and better opportunities. This translates into perseverance.

Mary Kay Ash herself set the tone of humble perseverance, and through hard work the company maintains that tone today.

Note

1. Based on the most recently published industry sales for the combined facial skin care and color cosmetics categories.

8

A Laurel Sat upon Wilts:
Innovate or Evaporate

MARY KAY INC. has surpassed the billion-dollar mark in global wholesale revenues every year since 1996. The company focuses on maintaining its connections to the independent sales force and sustaining the incredible loyalty of its millions of customers. thereby sustaining the healthy market share it has earned in both skin-care and color cosmetics. But its efforts don't end there.

Dating back to the days when Mary Kay Ash mimeographed a newsletter for the independent sales force, the company has always kept communications channels open. By the time the Internet initiatives were launched in 1996, the company had tailored its programs to meet the needs of the independent sales force using the new technology. By 2001 the company's Internet sites were receiving nearly 100 million page views per month.

The secret of Mary Kay's success is as complex as the company itself. Company leaders understand that without the independent sales force, these kinds of innovations would be virtually impossible. The company's culture and values create a platform for change that is based on relationships of trust. The emphasis on innovation at all levels of the organization means that the company can bring new ideas and processes to market at the speed of light. The interesting thing, though, is that no single group can take credit for this success. It is the result of all the parts of this complex, innovative machine working together.

This leads to the link that exists between each of the nine keys that drive sustainable success. Each one plays a role in sustaining the soul of the organization. Each one must be maintained if the level of innovation is to remain high.

Innovation

Innovation is a critical component of new-product success. When correctly managed, it contributes enormous excitement to the organization and greatly enhances the appeal of products to customers.

At the same time, innovation without solid direction can be a waste of effort and money. Innovation must be driven by carefully articulated goals. In direct sales, for example, innovation must lead to affordable products, offer quick and obvious results to the consumer, and be readily understood and explainable by the independent sales force.

The search for innovation must be conducted on multiple fronts. It includes, for example, in-house research and development, the purchase or license of innovation from an individual entrepreneur or company, and research collaboration with another entity.

Mary Kay's recently introduced "Calming Influence" product is a good case study of multitrack innovation in action. In 1996 Mary Kay Global Research and Development decided to pursue several high-potential ingredients and products in the skin-care area. One of the things it tested was a product to calm and soothe itchy, irritated skin—whether the cause was razor burn, windburn, exposure to household irritants such as dishwashing detergent, or some other cause. Mary Kay scientists launched a technology investigation that spanned in-house development, the licensing of patented technology, and the use of pharmaceutical ingredients. Concurrently, other Mary Kay scientists began to explore ways to measure product performance.

Mary Kay Inc.'s in-house development team utilized literature and patent searches and industry and supplier information. Botanical extracts showed the most promise, and a number of extracts reported to possess anti-irritant, calming, and soothing properties were identified. Researchers investigating licensing possibilities identified a patented ingredient that became the leading candidate. Numerous botanical extracts, blends of botanical extracts, and the licensed ingredient were evaluated by using two different test methods. The best-performing botanical extract blend then was tested against the licensed ingredient, and both were found to be equally effective in cell culture and panel tests.

At that point both approaches were assessed by using the innovation parameters discussed above, and the in-house innovation was found to be the more appropriate. Both technologies offered equally quick and obvious results; however, the licensed technology was very expensive and, because of its "chemical-sounding" name, was not as appealing and understandable to the consumer as was the in-house botanical extract blend.

Based on the in-house botanical blend, Mary Kay's Calming Influence, incorporating that blend, was launched in 2001. This highly innovative product has garnered rave reviews and impressive user testimonials and is on the way to becoming one of the best-selling Mary Kay products.

Eyes and Ears

Bill Gates, the chairman of Microsoft, once was asked in an interview what he feared most when it came to his competition.

"The next Bill Gates," he said.

This was not an egotistical remark but a capsule summary of what he had done to create one of the most successful companies in the world. He had built an organization in which every individual was part of the creative process. Gates was recognizing the power of innovation.

Companies that fail to innovate cease to exist. Sustainable success is the result of constantly becoming something different, as dictated by the future business environment. Mary Kay Ash realized that her company not only had to be capable of responding rapidly to unforeseen changes in the marketplace, it also had to be adept at anticipating the future.

Mary Kay focused the last two decades of her life on replicating herself and fostering more "Mary Kays" out in the world: the Independent National Sales Directors. More than 180 have reached this pinnacle in the Mary Kay sales force today, and they are motivators and leaders who continue to inspire the independent sales force as Mary Kay Ash did. But they are also on the front lines of innovation, the eyes and ears of what the marketplace will be calling for next. Among their many roles, the Independent National Sales Directors help keep the company future-oriented and focused on identifying the products that people are likely to want next.

Communication Fosters Innovation

Dr. Myra Barker's official area of responsibility is "anything that can touch a product." As executive vice president for global marketing/global research and development, she is responsible for marketing, product safety, quality, regulatory issues, and a host of other areas.

Although she was trained as a scientist, her days in the laboratory are long since over, and the way she now spends her time is a telling indicator of the kind of organization Mary Kay Inc. is today. Barker operates in a world without boundaries. On any given day she might be working with a team of Independent National Sales Directors, interfacing with a group of customers, or dialoging with other cosmetics industry leaders. Her contacts are diverse, and purposefully so: A company benefits enormously any time a leader can move comfortably among all the functional areas and disciplines of the organization.

As she sat in her lab office one afternoon a number of years ago, Barker had a lot on her mind. She was working her way through numerous letters and memos when the ringing of the phone broke her concentration. The call was from an executive search firm in New York. The search consultant told her that he was attempting to find and recruit an individual for a very special position. In fact, he said, that position was perhaps the most sought after in the cosmetics industry.

Barker knew what was coming next but played along. After a while the consultant confided to Barker that she was the top candidate for the job even though the candidate firm's management had never met her. Barker asked for details on the position and then added one seemingly innocuous question: "What about working with the field?" How much time does the research director for this firm spend working with the field?

The answer came back: This research director spends *no* time working with the field. The recruiter went on to explain that the research laboratory at the firm was one of the most advanced at any company in the world. That—plus the fact that this was one of the most prestigious positions in the industry—should definitely pique Barker's interest. Or so the consultant evidently thought.

He was not prepared for her response. "I spend a great deal of my time working with our Independent Beauty Consultants, Sales Directors, National Sales Directors, and retail customers," Barker told him. "It's the lifeblood of our work. It's the way we are able to excel at creating exceptional products. I appreciate your call, but your position is simply one that I would not be interested in."

The consultant didn't understand her reasoning. He reiterated his offer, and Barker again declined. He called back later in the day, and once again Barker declined. There were multiple reasons for Barker's decision, of course. But by her account, one of the more compelling was that she knew how successful innovation occurs and knew that it depends in part on getting out and around and being in the midst of new ideas. Staying in the lab all day, even a wonderfully equipped lab, is not likely to lead to products that customers embrace.

Innovation: The Lifeblood of the Company

It's possible to learn a great deal about the health of a company—whether a small family-owned business or a Fortune 100 giant—by studying the mix of the products it offers. If they are all tired, staid, and uninteresting products, it's quite likely that the company is entering or is already well into a time of difficulty. If, in contrast, there's a balance between the old, the relatively new, and the brand-new products, the future prospects of that firm are likely to be excellent.

In my work as a strategist I have been astounded by how few organizations really understand this issue. When most people think of Mary Kay cosmetics, they tend to think of the line of skin-care products that first brought the company to prominence four decades ago. But that's only a small part of the larger story that has grown up around it.

Today product improvements and innovations aren't just welcome, they are expected. The company pushes hard to secure its position (niche) between upscale specialty store brands and mass-market brands. As a result, Mary Kay has several comfortable market niches.

"A cosmetics company doesn't thrive for 40 years unless it is able to do both very well—create classics and constantly innovate," explains Dr. Barker. "We prefer to use our innovative power and creativity to force competitors to respond to us instead of the opposite. This is an extremely competitive business, and followers don't do well on a long-term basis."

Corporate Structure Drives Creativity

Innovation, narrowly defined, happens in the labs, test cells, proving grounds, and wind tunnels. But it also begins in and is sustained by organizational support structures far away from the lab.

One such support structure is the senior executive team. Barker tells a story about the time an outside consultant was hired to work with that team. The consultant administered individual evaluations to determine each executive's predispositions. The test involved a four-square grid, with the lower-left corner indicating a basic personality that liked stability and hated creativity and the upper-right corner indicating (1) a high tolerance for disruption and uncertainty and (2) high levels of creativity. With only one exception, the executive team came out in the upper-right quadrant—the one indicating high levels of flexibility and a desire to think creatively. "I've never seen this at a company before," said the consultant. "Normally, I find a lot of balance between the different areas, but never have I discovered a company with such a focused executive team, especially one so focused on creativity."

This translates into an openness to new ideas, which obviously bears on the company's ability to innovate successfully. Company leaders take a proactive stance in assessing possible changes in the customer needs communicated to them by the independent sales force and in communicating those needs to the people directly responsible for creating programs, practices, and products. *Intelligence* (in the information-gathering sense of the word) is highly valued. It is analyzed and acted upon.

As was indicated above, the Independent National Sales Directors also play an influential role in the creative process. One high-performing group, the Inner Circle, is called upon in a formal and systematic way for assistance with the creative process. The company's management team frequently asks the Inner Circle to gather in Dallas so that its members can present ideas to, solicit feedback from, and otherwise interact with that group. "To me," says Dr. Barker, "our interactions with these key leaders are another of Mary Kay's wisdoms we carry forth."

In addition to the Inner Circle, there are other Independent National Sales Directors who are involved in the process according to their expertise. There are advisory groups for both sales and marketing, for example, and those groups are engaged with almost every new product and sales idea. Eligible members serve on a rotating basis.

Within the company there are teams designed to encourage listening, action, and innovation at all levels. One of the early initiatives developed in the company was CAT, or creative action teams. Today the company uses strategic, cross-functional, and high-performance teams to do the innovative thinking.

As at most companies, strategic teams are formed to address a specific problem. For example one team, the Phoenix Project, addresses supply chain improvements. Launched in 1999, this project team is making a long-range and systematic effort to review every step in the product-delivery system from its conception to its delivery to an Independent Beauty Consultant. Again, the explicit agenda is to look for opportunities to innovate and improve on established practices.

The innovative process at Mary Kay therefore is multipronged. Yes, it involves people in white coats in laboratories, the sorts of people you think of first when you think of innovation. But it also includes an open and inquisitive executive corps, inside and outside advisory boards, and internal teams focused on specific strategic goals. Finally, it calls upon the entire organization to participate in the innovative process. On a regular basis, people across the company hear that every individual's contribution is important.

The outcome of all of these efforts is dramatic: an organization that is continuously innovating, improving both its products and its services, and embracing change as a path to the future. In management publications this is what is called a "learning organization." That means that this is a firm that can bring to bear all its intellectual firepower—executives, employees, independent sales force, and customers—on the challenge of understanding the future. The result? *Organizational knowledge.*

Knowledge Creation Is the Result of Organizational Learning

As Figure 8–1 shows, the Mary Kay organization is all about organizational learning and the creation of knowledge. It is the knowledge that the staff creates as a team that provides the foundation for what the firm and its products must become in order for the company to sustain its success.

"This continuous feedback loop from the knowledge process of each step is what keeps us competitive in our industry," said Dr. Barker. "The Mary Kay Ash concept of shared knowledge has made this process workable in our organization."

With obvious satisfaction, Barker comments further on the success of these concepts and on one in particular, known within the organization as marketing to a unit of one:

> One of Mary Kay Ash's most important sayings was, "When I meet someone, I imagine her wearing an invisible sign that says, 'Make me feel important!'" In product development and marketing we've developed this saying into a guiding principle we've used for many years.
>
> Dick Bartlett was the first to name this principle marketing to a unit of one. Every woman—whether an Independent Beauty Consultant or a consumer—wants products, marketing

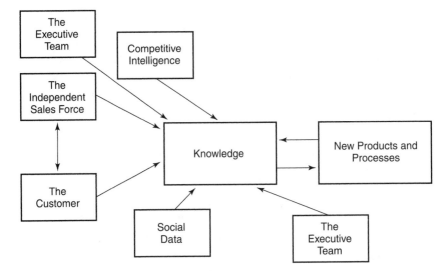

Figure 8-1. Continuous feedback loop.

information, and programs tailored to her individual needs. The challenge in a very large organization is providing personalization and choice for nearly a million Beauty Consultants and millions of consumers throughout the world without creating an impossibly large inventory burden for the individual Beauty Consultant.

In the early 1980s, when we first introduced skin type–specific skin-care formulas, we needed a way for the Independent Beauty Consultant to recommend these products to the customer. We introduced a three-part paper form known as the Skin Care Profile. This device allowed each customer to answer five simple questions that would lead to the correct product recommendations. It also enabled the Independent Beauty Consultant to individualize each customer's skin-care program by recommending customized skin-care products to address specific needs such as fine lines, dark pigment spots, acne blemishes, sunburn, and dark circles under the eyes.

We've distributed millions of these Skin Care Profiles over the years and have now made them available to Beauty Consultants over the Internet. A similar device for color cosmetics called a "Looks Card" allows a Beauty Consultant to recommend a complete, customized "look" to a customer, with product samples of lip, eye, and cheek color attached to the card. The Beauty Consultant also can customize brochure, postcard, and e-mail messages to her customers through the Preferred Customer Program mailings.

The key to all these programs designed to market to a unit of one is the fact that Mary Kay Independent Beauty Consultants truly know their individual customers. Because of that specific, first-hand knowledge, a Beauty Consultant can tailor her product presentation to each customer. Our job is to help the Beauty Consultant focus on each customer to make her feel important.

Innovate—Don't Evaporate

Dr. Barker believes that putting all these things together is one of the most difficult tasks a management team has to accomplish. "You have to remember," she says, "that we've been through a number of major market shifts, including some significant changes in our independent sales force. Add to that the frequent changes in consumer needs, and we have had to master being good at changing."

Barker and her teams strive to be one of the key links between what happens in the research lab and what they hear from the independent sales force. They also work closely with the marketing teams. Their collective job is to figure out where the consumer's desires will be in the future and how to get there first with the right products.

The history of Mary Kay Inc. is in part a story of product innovation. The following timeline captures that story, beginning with the recent past:

Product Innovation Milestones

2001   Velocity® products for the young market
2000   TimeWise® products
1993   Skin revival system

1988 Nail care
1985 Color cosmetics based on cool and warm colors to coordinate with skin tone measurements
1984 Foundations based on skin tone measurements made by thousands of Independent Beauty Consultants
1982 Body care
1981 Limited-edition products
1980 Basic skin care reformulated for all skin types
1978 First specialized skin-care products
1963 Original formula: one skin type

Barker notes that today many of the company's newest products are coming as a result of advances in technology. Many of these products are being developed in Mary Kay's own product laboratories and by its in-house scientists.

Breadth of Product Line

One corporate objective, the results of which show up in the timeline above, has been the gradual broadening of the Mary Kay product line. The creation of the TimeWise line of products is an excellent case in point.

In the later 1990s the company recognized that a number of socio-graphic changes were occurring in the marketplace. Increased hours spent in the workplace and a changing pace of life meant that the time demands on Mary Kay's customers were increasing. That drove a need to take the formerly five-step skin-care process and compress it in such a way that all five functions remained but required fewer steps.

At the same time, there was a race within the industry to come up with products that reduced the signs of aging.

In response to those two challenges Mary Kay Inc. introduced TimeWise products. This line reduced the skin-care process to three steps and also provided some unique age-fighting benefits that were documented through comprehensive clinical and laboratory testing. The company provided Independent Beauty Consultants with statistical results and impressive clinical before-and-after photos of "real people" who used the product, as opposed to already beautiful models.

The TimeWise line was an instant success. The two TimeWise products quickly became the company's number one and number two best-selling products. TimeWise was granted a patent in September 2002, and the company is planning to extend this revolutionary discovery to other products for the face and body. At the same time, the traditional five-step product line has continued to sell well. In many cases innovation translates into a "cannibalization" of existing product lines. So far this has not been an issue with the TimeWise line.

The Next Innovation Challenge: Managing Change

A lot of companies are fairly good at creating products, but not all of those companies are successful in more general terms. Beginning with the major changes in the early 1980s, the Mary Kay executive team realized it had to not only be great at creating new products and processes but also be great at getting the entire company, including the independent sales force, to adopt them.

"Changing demographics and changing products meant we had to handle a lot of issues at once," says Myra Barker. "Early on, a skin-care class was planned to last for two hours and used at least five different products. A changing consumer profile meant that we had to change that to two or possibly three products and also cut out time, in some cases down to 20 minutes." In addition, the company saw the need to help Beauty Consultants evolve their inventory so that it would not be made obsolete by the company's increasingly rapid pace of innovation.

The Mary Kay team developed an approach that targeted two key ideas. First, they made sure that they introduced the new products to the top sales force members first. This translated into providing information and samples to the Independent National Sales Directors early in the process. The second thing was to make sure that the change was driven through the entire independent sales organization within a very short period.

When President of Global Sales and Marketing Tom Whatley says that Mary Kay Inc. is one of the "top marketing companies in existence," he is referring to these kinds of effective connections; in other words, a network that is one of the best in the world at communicating with its independent sales organization. The company has developed numerous vehicles that allow it to custom design each initiative to suit the task.

In addition to new technology, more traditional communications channels, and the ambitious Seminar, Mary Kay developed two annual meetings: an annual Leadership Conference for all Independent Sales Directors and a series of regional meetings for the entire independent sales force. Both the Leadership Conference and the Career Conference are planned carefully to coincide with strategic product changes during the year.

The end result is twofold: At the Leadership Conference the company can communicate the upcoming year's plans to the top tier of its independent sales force. At the Career Conference the corporate staff comes into direct contact with the entire independent sales force as it literally blankets the United States in a two-week period. The rhythm of these meetings allows for reasonably painless and seamless learning, and both groups—corporate staffers and members of the independent sales organization—stay abreast of what's happening almost as soon as it's happening.

Dr. Barker is quick to confess that the company has to work harder to incorporate still more innovation-nourishing processes within the larger organization. She says her teams have learned that each new product launch provides a new learning experience, which underscores the fact that *there's always more to learn.* They put their newly acquired knowledge to use with each new rollout and immediately start looking for the next lesson.

Is there outside validation of the success of Mary Kay's efforts to innovate and drive change? Yes. For example, in 2001 Mary Kay Inc. received the Industry Innovation Award given by the Direct Selling Association (DSA) for its Internet personal Web site programs. As was noted in previous chapters, this innovation grew out of lessons learned from earlier innovations.

More than a decade earlier—in 1990—Mary Kay Inc. won the same award for its introduction of the Preferred Customer Program, which allowed the corporation to produce custom marketing materials for every participating Independent Beauty Consultant. This system was lauded not only for its marketing genius but also because it solved another problem. Before the implementation of the Preferred Customer Program, if an Independent Beauty Consultant stopped operating her business, her customers might be lost in the shuffle before they found another Beauty Consultant.

With the advent of the Preferred Customer Program, participating Independent Beauty Consultants could ensure that their selected customers would remain connected through another participating sales force member. The result was the retention of millions of customers who otherwise would have been left without easy access to their favorite products.

Based on this learning—and, as noted in earlier chapters, based on the common bond of trust that exists between the company and its independent sales force—the Mary Kay organization in 1996 began planning its approach to the Internet. Thus, there is a *lineage* of innovation—a sequence of new ideas, products, and procedures—that keeps the company both stable and forward-looking.

Sometimes It Starts at the Top

It's important to call on the entire organization for great ideas. It's also important to recognize that great ideas sometimes take root at the top of an organization. That is exactly what happened when the company's chairman, Richard Rogers, recognized an opportunity disguised as a problem.

What Rogers realized was that unlike the sales of retail-oriented companies, sales of Mary Kay's cosmetics products tended to drop substantially during the November–December time period each year. Apparently, people's discretionary dollars were being diverted in other directions during the holiday season.

In the early 1980s Rogers began investigating ways to reverse that situation. "What if we came out with a limited-edition line for each year's holiday period?" he asked. The team set out to investigate the idea and came up with a succession of limited-edition products that were targeted toward the holiday gift-giving season. For example, they developed special packaging for fragrances and men's products and also came up with unique children's gifts for the period. The result? More than two decades of increased sales in a formerly quiet season as well as increased customer satisfaction. It all happened because Mary Kay's leaders were willing to look at present practices with a critical eye, dig deep to innovate, and support an innovation to help it gain acceptance.

The Importance of Innovation

Companies that experience sustainable profit and growth are companies whose leaders understand the importance of innovation. It is not an issue of innovating for the sake of innovating. Rather, it is a matter of anticipating customers' needs and innovating quickly and effectively enough to meet emerging customers' demands.

Mary Kay Inc. is blessed with these qualities and skills. The company values—and therefore benefits from—innovation and creativity.

9

God, Family, Career: Foster Balance

GREAT INSTITUTIONS STRIKE a balance between God, family, and career.

These three words sound somewhat old-fashioned to modern ears. We have learned to downplay words that we think might be offensive or off-putting to a subset of the population, and to some extent that sensitivity is a good thing: There's no justification for imposing a particular creed or denomination on a heterogeneous workforce.

But sometimes when we give up using certain words, we risk giving up the concepts that lie behind those words. We forget that many of our great institutions—educational, governmental, social, and philanthropic— began as institutions with religious values. We overlook the fact that many of our great commercial institutions were established on a strong foundation of *principles*.

We no longer pray in public schools, and we no longer talk much about God in the workplace. Nevertheless, it's apparent that many of the companies that have done well in the last century have been those whose founders recognized the value of *balance* in the lives of their workers. In some of these companies the legacy of the founders' religious faith is still very much in evidence. Many of America's most successful companies—Acipco, one of the largest pipe companies in the world; J.C. Penney; Interstate Batteries of America; and many others—were founded by people who put their faith above all else and created workplaces where they could live out their beliefs. Those legacies are still in place today. The very best among those companies created a work environment in which people had the freedom to live out the priorities of God first, family second, and career third.

The Golden Rule is at the core of those legacies. It is a principle that guides relationships and mutual obligations among people. Not surprisingly, many principle-based organizations, which include many of the "best to work for" companies, are run in part on the basis of the Golden Rule as well as the other principles that govern human relationships.

This is certainly true at Mary Kay Inc. At the Mary Kay Ash memorial service after her death in November 2001 the primary focus was not on the global company she had built, the philanthropic work she had supported, or her other remarkable achievements. Instead, the focus was on her *faith* and how it not only enabled her to do great things in the business world but also influenced her relationships with every person she met.

Simply put, Mary Kay's business philosophy was the Golden Rule and a clear set of priorities: God first, family second, and career third. At the outset she set out to make this belief system a central part of her business, an objective she achieved to a remarkable extent.

Both clergy and lay speakers at the memorial service pointed out how Mary Kay Ash relied on her faith to get her through tough times as well as to keep her centered after she achieved great success. (Great success, as we know, has been known to throw even the most stable people off balance.) The Baptist and Methodist ministers who spoke, as well as the lifelong friends, business colleagues, and family members who offered observations, celebrated Mary Kay's lifetime of faith and commitment to principled leadership.

Dick Bartlett had the opportunity to watch Mary Kay practice "God, family, career" over the years. He comments on the way the company's founder consistently lived out her priorities over the years:

Candidly, I have experienced a lot of difficulty establishing balance in my life. And unfortunately, I am not alone in my workaholic ways. Again, I marvel at how Mary Kay Ash understood our basic need for a prescription for life's priorities. Perhaps this was because Mary Kay recognized workaholic tendencies in herself, which were the flip side of her awesome capacity and dedication. I believe she did strike an effective balance in her life, though, and once she had figured it out, she always considered it a top priority to help others achieve more harmonious lives.

Mary Kay's message was that you must stop from time to time. You must find time to restore your faith, love your family, care for others, smell a pink rose. That is the meaning behind "God first, family second, career third." She would go on to explain that, in that order, everything works—but out of this sequence, nothing works.

I can recall many an investment banker coming away from a meeting with Mary Kay and whispering to me, "She doesn't really believe that, does she? You can't run a billion-dollar business that way, can you?" These bankers had no clue as to how wrong they were. The answer in both cases was an emphatic yes.

Mary Kay demonstrated a lifelong deep faith in her God. But it's important to note that she never sought to impose her faith, her belief in God, on others. She came to understand that her global family embraced many faiths. And although she preferred to use the word God, she understood that when it came to people and countries that held different beliefs, the word faith could be substituted.

The words matter far less than the ideas. God first. Family second. Career third. Like so many of her precepts, it works as well today as it did in 1963.

While Mary Kay was open about her personal faith, she did not use her position in the company as a way to proselytize on behalf of her faith. She prayed, read the Bible, and faithfully worshipped God. She always spoke about the importance of religion in her life. When television's 60 *Minutes* came to interview her and Morley Safer asked Mary Kay if she wasn't just "using God," she looked Safer squarely in the eye and said, "I sincerely hope not. I hope instead that God is using me."

Balance

Mary Kay Ash grew up at a time when there was an unforgiving double standard that worked to the disadvantage of women. In most settings women were criticized for working even when they desperately needed to work. And when they did have a job, if they took time off from work to participate in a rite of passage such as a child's grade-school play or Little League game or even to deal with a medical problem, that decision was frowned upon.

Mary Kay had come to the realization that there was an expectation that women would not "make the commitment" to excellence on the job if they had children at home. And in fact, there were situations—lots of them—in which an extraordinary time commitment was required of anyone who wanted to advance in a company. In many cases men and women alike were expected to sacrifice family in order to move up the corporate ladder. Many companies, moreover, practiced an "up or out" policy: If you wouldn't or couldn't make the all-out commitment to climb the ladder, you eventually would lose your job.

Early in her life Mary Kay Ash was faced with the daunting challenge of being a single parent working desperately to create a better life for her young children. She knew first-hand the constant tension between her duties as a mother and her work responsibilities. She also recognized that many of the women she worked with were equally torn. Either you put your children first or you put your job first. You couldn't do both, and you certainly couldn't hope to "have it all."

In her period of service on other companies' payrolls Mary Kay had come in contact with countless people who had sacrificed family for career. This broke her heart, she later said, because she knew the terrible toll this choice took on the members of those families. Perhaps more than anything else, therefore, Mary Kay wanted to found a company where women could have opportunities that allowed them to nurture family relationships.

That's the spirit behind the current mission statement of the company. When that statement affirms that Mary Kay's mission is to "enrich women's lives," it speaks to the concept of a life in balance. It's the same balance that is captured in the phrase "God first, family second, career third."

As the seeds of her independent sales force began to sprout and take root, balance was the priority that many women picked up on. It was precisely what the founder hoped they would hear, and in subsequent years she spent a tremendous amount of time coaching women in ways to strike an appropriate balance. While she understood how difficult this was, Mary Kay did everything she could to make both the independent sales force and corporate employees the beneficiaries of her thinking.

Many people standing outside of Mary Kay Inc. and looking in conclude that the desire to make a lot of money is what drives the independent sales forces and, by extension, the company. In her third and final book, *You Can Have It All*, Mary Kay Ash contradicts that interpretation, explaining what really propels her company, at least from her perspective. She argues that a preoccupation with money and career is *not* the path to a happy life.

When Mary Kay suggests to a woman that "you can have it all," she's not really talking about money or career. She's talking about true success in life, which involves balancing faith, family, and work. "My definition of success," she writes, "would include living a balanced life. Balance means advancing your career up to, but not past, the point where it interferes with your happiness and relationships. Worthy advancement does not promote neglect of your husband and children. Nor should you work to the point where your health is endangered either physically or mentally."[1]

Let's look at the three priorities in their order of importance, as Mary Kay Ash saw it.

God First

Mary Kay Ash made it perfectly clear that she was a woman of faith. By so doing, she placed herself in the tradition of the New Testament's Book of James. In that book believers are called to show their faith by their works.

Mary Kay Ash often said that what was important was not what you say but what you do. She believed that the most powerful sermons ever preached were conveyed by actions rather than words.

She also believed that "right behavior" would produce unexpected results. That is, she believed that a commitment to right behavior, such as seeking the best for others, would produce other benefits. She often said that if you seek the best for others, the profits will follow. That principle pervades many scriptures, including the Book of Deuteronomy, which suggests that living God's principles produces blessings.

In almost every case the relationship principles espoused by Mary Kay are based on biblical wisdom, which might be defined as understanding the way things are supposed to be. This is the wisdom upon which Mary Kay built her organization, and it is the wisdom possessed today by the National Sales Directors, numbering some 180 women, who lead the independent sales force in the United States. Nearly all these leaders grew their businesses under Mary Kay's personal tutelage.

In the current global expansion efforts the company makes a strong effort to export key aspects of the Mary Kay philosophy internationally. It turns out that many of the Mary Kay principles do apply cross-culturally. Dr. Myra Barker recalls attending a Mary Kay Seminar in Russia, where she encountered a Siberian "Queen of Sales," her family, and her sister consultants, all of whom had traveled nine hours in order to attend. Barker listened in amazement, she says, as the Queen of Sales invoked Mary Kay Ash's values with passion and eloquence. "That was," she says today, "one of the most moving scenes I can recall in more than two decades."

One of the corporate officers attending the Seminar in Mexico recalls the heartfelt words of the husband of one of the independent sales force members there. The husband talked about how his wife's business had changed their lives. He spoke of his pride in being associated—even indirectly—with a woman like Mary Kay Ash. As I discovered during my many visits to Mary Kay headquarters, there are literally thousands of such stories. Collectively, they argue strongly that the priorities established by Mary Kay Ash in Texas many years ago are relevant to and welcomed by cultures around the world.

Mary Kay liked to spotlight the biblical idea of "fruitfulness" as it is presented in the Book of Proverbs, for example, in Proverbs 3:1–2: "My child, do not forget my teaching, but let your heart keep my commandments, for they will provide a long and full life and they will add wellbeing to you."[2] The wisdom of this text includes the promise of success. But note that the blessing is one of a *good life*; no particular earthly riches are implied. Another relevant message comes from Proverbs 24:27: "Establish [or prepare] your work outside and get your fields ready; afterward build your house."

One of the things that Mary Kay most enjoyed autographing was a dollar bill. This may sound like it runs against the "God first" creed that she espoused, but when handed a dollar, she would always inscribe it with the phrase "Matthew 25:14–30," referring to the biblical story known as the Parable of the Talents. In this parable the Lord expresses his satisfaction with the servant who turns his five "talents" (a type of currency) into ten and his dissatisfaction with the servant who buries his talents in the ground and earns nothing from them.

Many women who have gone on to earn stellar incomes have said that they treasured the dollar inscribed by Mary Kay Ash and found it to be a source of inspiration as they worked their way toward success.

Family Second

The second priority established by Mary Kay was that of family. Some people live to work; others work to live. Some have little choice one way or the other. Most of us know of companies—even early in the twenty-first century—that still expect their people to sacrifice everything for their careers. At such companies failure to put the job first often is perceived as a lack of commitment.

During her life Mary Kay Ash lost one husband who simply walked out on her. She lost another to a heart attack and a third to cancer. She left a career in which she had excelled because she couldn't tolerate the injustice she had experienced solely because she was a woman. But as with everything else in her life, she did not let the disappointments of her personal and professional life, however large, stand between her and what was truly important: family. In fact, she made her family her reason to succeed.

Some people have excuses; others have reasons. Mary Kay could have cited a lot of excuses—*good* excuses—for not being family-focused. By her early twenties, she had already shouldered tremendous responsibility and seen painfully difficult times. In her early childhood, when her mother worked long hours to support the family, and then as the sole supporter of three young children, she often had little money and less time. In her working life, when she came home from the office at the end of the day, her home workday was just beginning. Yet she found ways to nurture her family.

Mary Kay had seen what demanding workplaces can do to women and their relationships with their families. That is why she ranked families so high in her hierarchy of values. In defining her company's mission as being to enrich women's lives, she took it as her and her company's personal challenge to make a difference in the world. At her memorial service, her son, Richard Rogers, said simply, "Mary Kay made this world a better place."

Michael Lunceford, senior vice president of government relations at Mary Kay, recently visited China. After that visit he received a letter from a university student who had heard him speak. The student is a recipient of one of the scholarships Mary Kay China sponsors. Notice, as you read this letter, how important the priorities of God, family, and work have become to this student and how, even though her exposure to the Mary Kay culture has been limited, she perceives wisdom in living her life this way:

Dear Mr. Michael Lunceford:

I'm one of the girls in Zhejiang University (China) who are lucky enough to get Mary Kay Scholarship in March this year. Thank you for your kindness.

At the end of the donation ceremony, I, as a part-time journalist, asked [the head of Mary Kay in Asia] Mr. K.K.

Chua a question about the future of Chinese women. It was very kind of you to praise me for my question and give me your business card after the ceremony.

As a young girl, I often think of my future and ask myself: What kind of life I should lead? I didn't find the answer until your presentation in the donation ceremony of the Mary Kay Scholarship. The philosophy of Mary Kay you introduced to us—building a successful business while living a balanced life—is really worthwhile to me.

Last week, I took part in a debate competition on campus. The topic was "Family or Career, Which Is More Important?" The viewpoint of our group is that family was more important. We used the philosophy of Mary Kay to support our viewpoint, and we finally won the competition! I am glad to see that more and more youths on campus share this philosophy with me.

I am greatly honored that Mary Kay chose my hometown Hangzhou as her head office in China. In my opinion, Hangzhou is the most beautiful and feminine city in China. I would be very glad to be your guide when you come to Hangzhou next time.

Thank you for reading my e-mail at an interval in your busy schedule. I am looking forward to making friends with you and hearing from you.

Yours sincerely,

Xie Li (Sherry)

It is apparent that in a very short time Mary Kay Inc. has had a tremendous impact on Xie Li's life. She not only embraces the idea of putting family before career, she is more than willing to debate the point. It also seems clear that the change will probably be long-term, that this young Chinese woman will order her life around these principles.

In story after story from Mary Kay's most successful National Sales Directors, the theme of spending quality time with husband and children, brother, mother, father, and sister is consistent and constant. Yes, she believed and asserted that women could have it all. And at the same time she counseled that "counting your money by yourself is no fun."

In other words, invest first in the really important things.

Career Third

One of the most interesting aspects of the career path Mary Kay Ash charted is that it easily could be described as the "impossible dream" business. She congratulated women for aiming for the impossible, and she emphatically wanted them to pursue and achieve their dreams.

As was noted above, she also believed in leading by example and showing people how to create balance in a complicated life. But sometimes setting the example for a growing and increasingly far-flung independent sales force meant biting off more than even Mary Kay Ash could chew.

One example occurred in 1975, when Mary Kay was concerned that the organization had become complacent. She decided that something had to be done to reignite the enthusiasm of the sales force. Someone suggested that she come up with some kind of a contest that would reinvigorate the sales organization. Mary Kay, thinking this over, knew that the kind of women who made up her independent sales force relished a challenge and would be willing to work to overcome it.

One thing led to another. Soon Mary Kay Ash was making the commitment to do what she consistently asked her independent sales force to do: book and conduct 10 skin-care classes in one week. In making this very public announcement she was challenging the entire independent sales organization to match her commitment. Of course, this captured the imagination of everyone in the larger organization: Could Mary Kay make her goal? Could they follow her lead?

Publicly, the founder was supremely confident. Privately, she expressed concern that she might fail to live up to her own challenge. She was well aware that although she had proved her skills at running a complicated and fast-growing company, when it came to actually going out and selling the product, she might be a little rusty. With some urgency she began boning up on product-related specifics, making sure she was up to date on both products and processes. Then the chairman rolled up her sleeves and began making phone calls to friends and neighbors. Would they be willing, she asked, to host a Mary Kay class in their homes, led by none other than Mary Kay Ash herself?

By the time her "commitment week" arrived, Mary Kay had no fewer than 20 classes scheduled. She conducted every class herself, and by all measures—including crossing the finish line—the week was a success.

The boss had taken a major risk. She had made a highly visible demonstration of her commitment to work and personal accomplishment. The effort achieved its ultimate goal of lighting a fire under the independent sales organization, and the sales organization soon was back on track.

A lot of people know how to tell others to embrace standards of excellence. Great leaders like Mary Kay set and achieve those high standards in their own lives. She not only practiced what she preached, she illustrated how "the speed of the leader is the speed of the gang." She challenged all her independent sales force leaders and staff members alike to remember this tenet. When it comes to an individual's commitment to his or her work, the only acceptable descriptor is *intense*. When it comes to the quality of that work, the only acceptable descriptor is *excellent*.

What it all boils down to is *purpose*. People who have a clear purpose in their lives tend to be much happier than are those who do not. Research reveals that people who are goal setters are happier than people who are not. People who assert some control over their destinies are healthier than people who do not. In the context of the priorities of God, family, and career, work can be an important source of self-fulfillment and personal accomplishment.

More Than a Pink Airplane

One day not too long ago, one of the students in the MBA program at the university where I teach—a student who also happens to be the procurement manager for one of the largest technology companies in the world—found out that I was writing this book. She sent me an e-mail encouraging me to talk with her mom, an Executive Senior Sales Director with Mary Kay. In the e-mail she recalled that she remembered waking up on Saturday mornings listening to a group of ladies singing, "I've got that Mary Kay enthusiasm down in my heart, down in my heart."

She also made a strange statement: Her mother was the proud possessor of a pink airplane.

I called her mother the same day. My first question was: "Surely your daughter's e-mail was mistaken. You really don't have a pink airplane, do you?"

"Yes," she replied, laughing. "I have a pink Cadillac *and* a pink airplane." She then went on to tell me the story.

While her husband was in dental school, she had worked as an assistant in a doctor's office to help support their four children. It was work she found stressful and unfulfilling. In a story that's repeated thousands of times in the company lore, a friend told her about Mary Kay Cosmetics, and she signed up. "Six weeks later, I had quit that job in the doctor's office," she says. "I had already surpassed my full-time salary with my part-time Mary Kay income." She continued to support the family during the remaining year and a half of her husband's dental education from her Mary Kay income.

In 1977, when Ruth Williams and her husband were divorced, she decided to pursue a dream she'd had since she was a child. She wanted to fly an airplane. She earned a pilot's license, and by 1979 she had purchased her very own airplane, a Piper 140.

As her Mary Kay business progressed, Williams decided that she wanted to paint the airplane pink. While the pink paint was being applied, she also came upon the idea of changing the N number on the aircraft that all airplanes registered in the United States must display. But the paint job was already under way, and a decision was needed pronto. She called the Federal Aviation Administration (FAA), the only agency that could authorize such an exception, and got into a conversation with an administrator there.

At first the administrator was somewhat discouraging. It might not be possible at all, she said. In any case, the process of getting an approval was likely to take at least six weeks. But as they chatted, the FAA employee discovered that Williams was a Mary Kay Sales Director.

"I'm a Mary Kay customer," said the woman. "Maybe we can get this expedited." Less than a week later Williams had her new N number—240 MK—officially okayed for her pink airplane. Now, more than two decades later, Williams flies her pink airplane everywhere.

"It's changed my whole family, and I have been blessed beyond my wildest imagination," she says of her association with Mary Kay Inc. She has seen firsthand the impact the company has on people's lives—not just her own but many others around her. "And a key reason," she says, "is that they live the ideals of God, family, and career."

God, Family, and Work

I mentioned earlier that in the past decade or so the business best-seller lists have hosted dozens of books with titles like *Why SOBs Win and Others Lose, You've Got to Be Number One, Looking Out for Number One, The Leadership Secrets of Attila the Hun,* and so on.

These are not books that you're likely to find in offices around the Mary Kay organization—except perhaps as examples of wayward thinking. Mary Kay Inc. subscribes to very different attitudes about people and about success. Keying off the strong beliefs of its founder, Mary Kay Inc. is a champion of women and of their families. Long before other companies woke up to the fact that women could make an enormous contribution to the success of their businesses if given the opportunity to strike and maintain a balance in their lives, Mary Kay Ash's company was out there, scooping up ambitious and talented women. It was providing them with a unique opportunity to make peace with God, enjoy their families, and be successful (monetarily and otherwise) in business.

Notes

1. Mary Kay Ash, *You Can Have It All,* Rocklin, CA: Prima Publishers, p. 5.
2. The New English Translation, 2001, Garland, TX: Biblical Studies Press, LLC (available at www.netbible.com at no cost).

10

Have a Higher Purpose

My primary motivation for going into business was to help women. I wanted to provide opportunities for them to create better lives.

— Mary Kay Ash

Almost everything Mary Kay Ash did in the founding and running of her company was animated by a sense of *higher purpose*. In other words, there was a core idea—or, more broadly, a view of the world—that moved the founder to behave the way she did. This is not an especially common starting point for a company, but it can be an extraordinarily powerful one. Henry Luce, for example, was appalled by the carnage of World War I and was convinced that the conflagration had arisen because people around the world simply didn't understand one another. He invented a new information vehicle—a weekly newsmagazine that he called *Time*—to promote mutual understanding on a worldwide basis.

In the last few years the idea of servant leadership has been put forward in many discussions involving corporate governance. At the heart of the idea is the concept of leaders acting as servants to their subordinates. This conveys the idea of putting the needs and goals of others in a superior position to one's own. This too is a powerful core idea or world view, but in real life servant leadership is a rare commodity.

Why? To answer this question in "Mary Kay vocabulary," most of us are more about "go get" than we are about "go give." Those familiar with the company will immediately recognize the trademarked term "go give" because it is used frequently in defining what Mary Kay Inc. is all about. When we tell the truth about ourselves—when we look in the mirror—most of us have to admit that we are out for ourselves. We do not wake up each day and ask ourselves, "What can I do for others today?" Instead, what we tend to ask is, "What can I do to advance my self-interest today?"

But the tension remains, the vague sense that there is more to life than just taking care of number one. That tension is fueled in part by the process of maturing. We take responsibility for the happiness of our spouses. We accept the responsibility of looking after our children and other family members. Yes, each of us is still front and center in our own minds, but gradually we accept broader responsibilities.

This tension, which I consider a positive force, is far less common in the workplace. Work tends to be transaction-oriented: Here's the deal: You get this; I get that. On to the next deal. In some corporate settings that's more or less the whole story. If you provide a good product at a fair price, you are fulfilling your unwritten contract with the public at large.

But as with most things in life, this issue is, or should be, more complicated. Corporations, like people, have to decide whether they are *givers* or *takers*. They have to decide if they have a higher purpose.

Aligning Purpose and Profit

If you look at organizations that do indeed act on a sense of their higher purpose, you find that that higher purpose always comes down to *seeking the best for others*. (Recall our discussions of the Golden Rule in earlier chapters.) This may take the form of lending a helping hand, providing financial guidance, or supplying a service such as training or education — or any one of an infinite range of specifics—but it boils down to the same thing: making someone else's life better.

Back to reality. If you look at most corporate initiatives, they are all about profit, either direct or indirect. In a lot of cases a company's involvement in a charity event would never occur if senior management did not think that the public relations and marketing benefits outweighed the direct costs.

But there is a different type of involvement that occurs at exceptional companies.

At those companies the higher purpose of seeking the best for others is lived out on a daily basis. Multiple screens are applied to each key question. People ask, "Will we make a profit if we go in this direction?" But they also ask, "Through this action, are we creating an environment in which people are valued?"

The answers to these questions are not mutually exclusive (or don't have to be). If you create a company in which people are valued, people will want to be associated with your company. In fact, some of the best people around will seek you out. And while a superior talent pool doesn't lead directly to profits, it is surely a nice building block to have.

The next thing that happens in your "people-valuing" organization is that those affiliated with it have a desire to share their experiences with others. They want their friends and family members, most of whom share their personal values, to know about your company and the way it treats people.

Somewhere along the line, filled with the confidence and gratitude that come with being valued in the workplace, people in your organization want to share themselves with those in need, including those outside the company.

Finally, the circle is closed. The larger community responds with gratitude to your company, which, through the selfless actions of its members, has demonstrated that it has the larger community's best interests at heart.

On a superficial level, of course, you can get there a lot faster by sponsoring a charity event, underwriting the local public radio station, or doing some other "good deed." (Once again, these are good things and need doing.) But there's a qualitative difference between the good will that grows out of a transaction (sponsoring, underwriting) and the good will that grows out of valuing people.

Make a Wish

Let's look sideways at a story that makes this point. It involves Mary Kay Inc. and a charitable organization called the Make a Wish Foundation. This story came to me from a former student who works for that nonprofit agency. Make a Wish partners with numerous donors and corporations to grant a wish to a child with a serious illness. Many of the children involved in the program are dealing with leukemia, cancer, and other life-threatening diseases. In 2002, the Make a Wish organization in Puerto Rico received a request from a young child with a very serious heart condition. Her wish? She wanted to go to Dallas and meet a woman named Mary Kay Ash.

It seems that the young girl's mother worked in television in Puerto Rico and had a Mary Kay business on the side. The child's needs, plus the demands of a stressful job, meant that her mom was often pushed to the point of exhaustion. Under the pressure of circumstances, the mother began building her Mary Kay business until finally she was able to stay home and work and at the same time devote more time to her daughter.

In her request to Make a Wish the little girl simply expressed a desire to go to Dallas and thank Mary Kay, whom she credited with making a difference in her life. She wanted to relate how much it meant to have her mother at home as she dealt with the trials and terrors of heart disease.

The trip never happened. Before she could come to Dallas, the girl, Maria Rivera, was placed on an active standby list for a heart transplant, which meant travel was forbidden. The company was prepared to roll out the red carpet for the child if and when she could fulfill her wish. Numerous people in the company wrote her, and gifts were sent. They found her a pen pal, the daughter of an Independent National Sales Director. Sadly, Maria lost her battle with heart disease. Just months after losing her daughter, Eugenia Rivera attended her first-ever Seminar in 2002, including a tour of the corporate headquarters building. "I felt Maria's presence so close to me in Dallas. When I walked into the Mary Kay Building, I broke into tears. Her dream was to go there. Now, by being there, I was making my own dream come true," Rivera recalls.

I cite this story, even with its sad ending, because it demonstrates the indirect but powerful consequences of operating with a higher purpose. The world gets changed for the better, and people out in that world know that it's your organization that has changed it.

In researching Mary Kay Inc. I spent a good deal of time reading a sampling of the thousands of letters that the company gets every month. Many are surprisingly intimate and moving. In almost every case there is a desire to go out and share with others the "enrichment" that each story-teller has experienced. This is not hype but heartfelt. Consistently, across the organization I encountered people who were eager to stand up and testify that the company's commitment to a higher purpose had been beneficial not only to them but also to those around them.

The Mary Kay Ash Charitable Foundation

In 1996 the Mary Kay Ash Charitable Foundation was created. In accordance with the organization's mission of enriching women's lives, the foundation focuses its activities on the areas of cancers affecting women and domestic violence. This twin focus reflects the needs of the Mary Kay population, which is a cross-section of the general public. Just like the rest of the female population in the United States—and around the world, for that matter—the women in the independent sales force may be victims of domestic violence or can be stricken with cancer.

One of the main priorities of the foundation is education. The foundation publishes a newsletter, *Heart To Heart,* that provides resource information for victims of violence and cancer as well as information about the foundation. The foundation has had tremendous grassroots support from Independent Beauty Consultants around the nation. Since its creation in 1996, it has supported cancer research, women's shelters, and education on these issues. In 2001, for example, the foundation made donations to 51 different women's shelters in the United States and funded a Public Broadcasting Service (PBS) documentary on the subject of domestic violence. The documentary, which will be aired on PBS through 2004, garnered the foundation and the company the prestigious Vision for Tomorrow award from the Direct Selling Association in 2002 for its work in shedding light on this issue. Among U.S. corporations, Mary Kay Inc. has become an outspoken advocate for the prevention of domestic violence.

On the foundation's Web site (www.mkacf.org) is a story that captured both my imagination and my emotions. The story, illustrating the challenges that cancer victims face, is that of the Mary Kay Independent Beauty Consultant Janne Catlett.

Janne Catlett

"Cancer can be difficult to talk about," says Janne Catlett. "It's not something that anyone should take lightly." The topic has come up more than she'd like over the past several years. Her mother died from cancer in 1992. Her stepmother lost her battle with breast cancer this year. Janne's first diagnosis came in 1997.

"I think people would be surprised at how much cancer is a part of our lives. It can happen to anyone, and those of us who've been through it once know how serious it is," says Janne. Recovery is practically a full-time job for Janne these days. To date, she's received 15 rounds of chemotherapy that send her body into an exhausting "crash" cycle the week after treatment. In one year's time, she has endured countless CAT scans, MRIs, bone marrow tests, and blood work tests that have turned her arms into pincushions.

"I'll endure anything right now to get better for my children's sake and mine," says Janne, who is the mother of two girls, ages 10 and 6. "Cancer has a way of changing your outlook on things. I can't wait for my girls to come home after school and give them a hug. I thought I had until forever, but suddenly, you get the message that it's not necessarily so. Cancer has been an awakening for me."

Janne's story is representative of the hundreds of other women associated with Mary Kay and the uncounted millions of women elsewhere who discover that they have this disease. In its pursuit of the higher purpose of the Mary Kay organization, the foundation attempts to help all who come looking for good answers and, of course, also seeks to educate the rest of us on both cancer and domestic violence prevention.

Giving and Expecting Nothing in Return

Mary Kay Ash believed that an exclusive focus on business was not good for a person or her career. Although she created many wealth-generation opportunities, she felt strongly that an obsession with wealth was neither positive nor healthy. She believed further that to be a complete person, an individual needed to live out the principle of a higher purpose in the lives of others.

In her view, giving was an excellent way to experience personal fulfillment. She avoided the idea of a simple quid pro quo—that giving should be linked directly to financial gain—but she truly believed that if you adopted the idea of giving to others, you would get back tenfold what you gave. One of her favorite sayings is the subject of an entire tape in the "Pearls of Wisdom" tape series that Mary Kay recorded in 1993: "All you send into the lives of others comes back into your own."

As a demonstration of that principle, Mary Kay once distributed a pin that was made up of two shovels, one larger than the other. She said the small shovel represented the things a person did in the life of another to help that person. The larger shovel represented the blessings that would come back into the life of the giver.

As one who has watched the impact of the Mary Kay philosophy on many lives over the last 30 years, Dick Bartlett has some unique insights into it. In the following paragraphs he observes how the company's success is linked to the higher purpose of changing lives for the better:

> *In my view, a company has to have a purpose beyond profit. This is essential to create and maintain the trust, motivation, and productivity of your workforce as well as the loyalty of your customers.*
>
> *I continue to be disturbed by the callousness among many CEOs toward their workforces, their customers, and the environment. My personal opinion is that we have a long way to go before most corporations pay more than lip service to higher purposes. And by the way, this isn't about money. I do not believe that return on investment and lofty shareholder value are the sole purposes of business. Legitimate profits, of course, must be*

earned so that enterprises can be sustainable. To my way of think-
ing, ideally there should be profits with a conscience.

I take some comfort from the fact that most Mary Kay
employees and the independent businesswomen of our sales
force leave their homes each day with the sure knowledge that
they are part of something great. They know Mary Kay is
changing the world for the better. They have meaningful par-
ticipation in the success of Mary Kay, either from inside the
company or in their independent businesses.

I mentioned previously the concept of "Go-Give." As a founding principle of the company, "Go-Give" was always at the center of everything Mary Kay Ash personally believed in and taught. That carried over to everything that was done in the context of the company. If an Independent Beauty Consultant was in a quandary about a choice between her Mary Kay career and another career, for example, Mary Kay Ash encouraged the individual to choose that which she wanted most. If it meant losing a talented Independent Beauty Consultant, that mattered little. The real issue was what was best for the individual at that point in her life. Through such actions, she set a standard for herself of "giving without expecting anything in return," and it was her heart's desire that her entire organization would live by that higher purpose.

Mary Kay Inc. has found many ways to reward high performers in the sales force financially. But to ensure that her organization kept its focus on a higher purpose, Mary Kay Ash also created an annual award that has nothing to do with money: the Go-Give Award. It is given each year to individuals in the sales force who give of themselves without expecting anything in return. It is today one of the most coveted awards among the many that the company hands out.

At the End of the Day

Is your company a giver or a taker?

Are the people within your company givers or takers?

Are you a giver or a taker?

I once had a conversation with a physician whose office was near the headquarters of a major international company. Many of this physician's clients worked for that company.

"They come into my office with all kinds of problems," the doctor told me, "but the real problem is that they are suffering from the stress that results from the negative, performance-oriented atmosphere at that company. I see it all—heart problems, high blood pressure, depression, and all sorts of ailments—in their employees. And it's clear that a large proportion of their physical problems can be traced right back to the awful environment at that company."

I dug a little deeper after that conversation. That company is famous—or infamous—as one that expects its employees to be willing to sacrifice everything for their careers. Family plans are subject to the whim of a manager. The company's charitable giving is based strictly on the potential for return in the marketing area.

In short, it's a dreadful place to work. Is it any wonder that this organization is known for strained relations between management and its people? Is there any doubt that a change in philosophy that refocused the company on a higher purpose—almost any higher purpose—would result in higher performance and profits for the firm?

At the end of the day people want to believe that they work for an organization that cares about them. They want to participate in something that is more than just making money. They want to leave the world better than they found it.

And somewhere down the line, yes, out the other side pops something called profit. You give, and sooner or later you receive—but as a fringe benefit. You lead—and win—by serving.

11

OK Never Does It:
You've Got to Be Great!

FOR THE UNINITIATED, a first encounter with Mary Kay Ash could hold some surprises.

"How are you today?" she would invariably say to someone whose path she crossed, whether she knew that person or not.

"Okay," that person might respond.

And that's when that person would get his or her first lesson in attitude. Mary Kay expected people to take an OK day and make it great. She expected people to take an OK *life* and make it great. "Acceptable" was not acceptable; you had to commit to being *great*.

Many Independent National Sales Directors talk about achieving what they thought were their ultimate goals, only to have the bar raised by Mary Kay herself. Make no mistake about it: Mary Kay was great at recognizing an accomplishment, but she was even better at using that accomplishment to set an even higher next goal for the individual. In many stories told by members of the independent sales force about Mary Kay Ash you hear about a success paired with a challenge: yesterday's achievement paired with a new goal.

Many times these goals and challenges had to do with sales targets, but not always. National Sales Director Wanda Dalby recalls that she was once encouraged politely to "learn to smile." Once Dalby had overcome that hurdle, she was encouraged to "learn to enjoy smiling."

You probably can guess the punch line in most of these stories. Most women challenged by Mary Kay to achieve an exceptional goal assumed they could not and then went right ahead and did it.

For Mary Kay the bumblebee was a symbol of achievement. Early in her working life she read that aerodynamically the bumblebee is an impossibility: It ought not to be able to fly. "But the bee doesn't know that," Mary Kay would say, "and so it flies anyway. It's the same way with women. They aren't supposed to be able to achieve these lofty goals, but they do it anyway."

As it turns out, for the members of the independent sales force this constant raising of expectations is every bit as meaningful as is the increased income that accompanies it. In many cases it's *more* meaningful because women who did not believe they were capable or talented enough become a powerful force in motivating other women to believe and behave the same way. This is precisely why Mary Kay's top independent sales force achievers are the preferred speakers at Mary Kay events: They are among the most articulate and dynamic motivators around. As Mary Kay Ash understood early on, those who have walked the walk talk the talk best.

Dick Bartlett says that Mary Kay was a genius at getting people to achieve their potential. "She would get them to commit to what might be perceived as a very low goal," he recalls. "Then she would personally challenge them to their next, higher goal. Ultimately, she would coach a person who thought she could never sell anything into achieving remarkable results."

The Commitment to Be Great

On most days the Mary Kay Inc. headquarters in Dallas is a study in measured and methodical operations. A few days a month, though, the picture changes drastically and there is a nearly frantic flurry of activity.

Those are the days when hundreds of new Independent Sales Directors descend on the headquarters building during their first day of new director education.

For one thing, there is almost always a commotion outside the building as groups of new Independent Sales Directors gather around a pink Cadillac that is strategically parked right in front of the main entrance. One after another, each waits her turn to pose in front of the pink Cadillac. Each tries to outdo her colleagues in striking the most dramatic pose in front of, or sometimes even draped across the hood of, the car. Of course, there are cameras at the ready to record the event.

I was a fly on the wall during one of those training sessions, watching the scene outside the building from the lobby. A Sales Director who had already had her picture taken in front of the car came in through the front door and then turned and watched her colleagues outside.

"It looks like 'commitment time' out there," I said to her.

"Yes," she replied. "We're all making a personal commitment about when we will earn our Cadillac."

About that time another one of the trainees came inside. She walked up and began chatting with us. It wasn't long before we learned what goal she had set for herself. "I made the commitment," she said confidently, "to have that car in time for my birthday."

The transition to Independent Sales Director is an important step for those who choose a Mary Kay business. It means that when their sales production warrants it, they are qualified to earn the use of the coveted pink Cadillac and that they can begin their leadership journey in earnest. "The Cadillac is not really the issue," the new Sales Director I was visiting told me. "It's about excellence and realizing your potential."

I asked about her background, and once again, as often happens when I ask that question of a member of the Mary Kay independent sales force, the answer was surprising. "I spent 25 years in teaching," she told me, "earned two master's degrees, and received good recognition for my work.

"Nevertheless, I became interested in the Mary Kay product and started looking into the business opportunity that it represented. I had been associated with many organizations that had a great mission statement, but when it came to 'walking the talk,' I found that most of them didn't measure up. That's why, as my interest in the business opportunity grew, I decided to check out this company Mary Kay thoroughly."

This former teacher did her homework. She went to the library, did some reading in the trade periodicals, and checked out some books by Mary Kay Ash. After that careful study she decided that this was a company that practiced what it preached. She seized the initiative: "I simply walked up to a woman who sold Mary Kay and told her I wanted to start my own Mary Kay business."

Gradually, she began learning about the company first-hand, and what she found confirmed her initial research (and overcame any residual skepticism). She decided that Mary Kay Inc. was different from all the other organizations with which she had been associated in that it lived the values it preached.

In her two short years with a Mary Kay business, she says, it has become clear that her association with exceptional people who set exceptional goals—and then *meet* those goals with help from others—has had a profound impact on her. And there's an unexpected satisfaction that one encounters along the way, she says: "I get to watch people change."

Although most of the personal accounts by the 12,000 women who have become Independent Sales Directors vary dramatically in their particulars, the themes of this former teacher's story are almost universal: an opportunity perceived and seized, lessons learned about oneself, the satisfaction of growing and watching others grow around you. You get to watch people change, beginning, of course, with yourself.

A People-Focused Organization Is a High Performer

If you had to chart the morale of a typical person pursuing a career at a typical company, that "career morale trajectory" might look something like Figure 11–1.

Typically, when people begin a career at a company, they are told about how employee-oriented the firm's management is and how there is great opportunity. But at most companies it doesn't take long for reality to

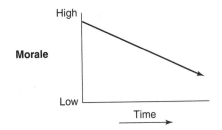

FIGURE 11-1. Career morale trajectory.

set in. You realize you were hired to do a job, and that is about it. As long as you show up for work on time and complete your assigned tasks—and, of course, the company doesn't go in the tank—you will get your modest annual raise. After you realize that the main objective of the firm is to maintain the status quo, your biggest personal challenge is to keep up your morale as you count down the days to retirement.

Ayn Rand, the author and philosopher, once said that the most demoralizing thing you can ask a person to do is mediocre work. In most cases, unfortunately, that's what companies ask for. Heaven forbid that you go to the office with an attitude of making a positive difference. At most companies that would be perceived as a threat to the status quo. It's not surprising, therefore, that for many people morale begins to decline the day (or week, or month, or year) they begin working at a new job.

At a very few companies the career morale trajectory looks different. People take up their new posts with the enthusiasm of new converts, and then they find that their need are met and their expectations are exceeded. Over their working lives, morale climbs more or less steadily, as illustrated in Figure 11–2.

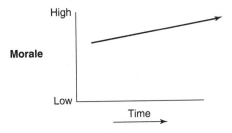

FIGURE 11-2. Effect of passing time on morale.

What's going on here? How can you have a company where morale goes up over the years rather than down? The secret lies in a concept that I call life scripts.

Success Begins with Changing One's Self-Concept

As we leave childhood and enter adulthood, every one of us has a life script. This is simply a set of attitudes that we have about ourselves. They can be positive or negative, but in either case they're powerful.

Life scripts are self-fulfilling. In other words, if we have written a life script for ourselves that says we "don't get along with people," we almost certainly will fail to get along with people. If our life script says that we are doomed to failure, we somehow will make sure that we fail. People who are dishonest are often that way because they are convinced that they cannot achieve an objective in the same way their peers do, by being honest and authentic. Therefore, they condemn themselves to a life of dishonesty and inauthenticity.

The good news is that, at least in my observation, bad life scripts can be rewritten. It requires commitment and a supportive context—family, workplace, and community—but it is possible to work out and live out a new script.

Often, during my visits to the Mary Kay headquarters, I would strike up conversations with employees who happened to be in the lobby for one reason or another. More often than not—surprisingly often, given that these were only casual conversations—they would wind up telling me their life scripts.

They didn't use this term. They used a term that I introduced in a previous chapter: the "I-story." And the reason I kept bumping into I-stories is that they're everywhere in the Mary Kay organization. If you have a discussion with the company's chief operating officer, he's very likely to tell you his I-story.

As I listen to these stories, I translate them into my own life script metaphor. In a situation where an employee's morale goes down over time, that employee generally is playing out his or her life script. Yes, most likely she finds herself in an undesirable work situation, but according to her life script, she really didn't deserve any better. Although she may complain about her circumstances, she rarely does much to change those circumstances. Why? Because in her heart she believes she's getting what she deserves.

At companies where morale increases, the circumstance is very different. It's possible that those companies hire more effectively, but I think that accounts for only a small proportion of the difference. The real difference is that at these companies people get to change their life scripts. They get to discover that they're competent rather than incompetent and valued rather than disposable.

How do they get there? I've already implied the answer in previous chapters: through positive relationships with the people around them. Changing a life script involves the active contributions of other people who want you to succeed and are willing to make investments in you. "Mentoring" has become a trendy concept in recent years among people who study management. What's mentoring if not an investment in one person by another?

What would happen if you could create what might be called a mentoring organization? Wouldn't a lot of life scripts get rewritten?

Discovering the Champion Within

Most people who go through basic training in the Army never forget the first day. From early in the morning to late at night you do nothing but run and do push-ups and sit-ups. At the end of that day most of the recruits find that they can hardly stand up and that their arm muscles are shaking uncontrollably.

At the time it feels like torture. If you volunteered for this, you can't imagine what inspired you to do so. You want out. You can't imagine going through this hell again tomorrow.

And yet you do. Gradually, your endurance goes up and the pain subsides. You start to look back on the first day and realize that it was one of the best days of your life. Not because you were exhausted and in pain, of course, but because you learned that your capacities far exceeded your expectations of yourself. You couldn't have imagined that you could do that many push-ups and sit-ups or run that far. You have a newfound confidence in your personal abilities. You look at new challenges very differently.

In talking with people at Mary Kay Inc., whether company employees or members of the independent sales force, you are struck by the high percentage who are articulate, disciplined, and enthusiastic. They give the impression of having always been that way. But that's not necessarily the case—even at the very top.

High Expectations Create Champions: Doretha Dingler

Take the case of Independent Executive National Sales Director Doretha Dingler, a top-ranking member of the Mary Kay sales force.

"I just wanted to marry the right man and have my 2.8 children," Dingler recalls with some amusement.

She has reason to be amused. Through her Mary Kay association, Dingler has rung up lifetime earnings of more than $9 million. She recently received the highest single monthly commission check ever received by an Independent National Sales Director: more than $100,000. By her own account a "rather ordinary" young woman from Athens, Texas, Dingler embodies what happens when someone is helped to rewrite his or her life script and discover the champion within.

Dingler got her exposure to Mary Kay Inc. just 18 months after the company was founded. "My original reason for getting involved in Mary Kay was the fantastic results I achieved on my skin with the product," she recalls. At that point—September 1965—there were no dollar signs or leadership inclinations in her script. There was just a yearning to "do something" with her time. She wasn't working, and her husband had graduated from college and was gainfully employed.

Dingler attended a Mary Kay event. She liked what she saw, and with very little deliberation and without much in the way of expectations she become involved in Mary Kay. Then her life started to get a little more complicated. "Nine months to the day after I had decided to become a Mary Kay consultant," she recalls, laughing out loud, "I had my first baby. No cause and effect there, of course."

The new mother put her career on the back burner for almost two years. Her sales volume tailed off. By 1968, just after her husband was transferred to Greenville, South Carolina, she received a termination letter from Mary Kay. "With all the moving and such," she explains, "I had let my Mary Kay activities go back to zero. But I did not want to lose my relationship with the company, and I really did not like the idea of this 'termination letter.' To be honest, it ticked me off. I had never been terminated from anything before. That's when I decided to show them that they were wrong to terminate me."

The episode served as a wake-up call, but Dingler was still at a bit of a disadvantage. She knew only two families in Greenville, South Carolina, and having and making contacts are integral to success in direct selling. But she persisted, and by 1969 she had reached the first leadership step toward becoming an Independent Sales Director.

"That's when the wheels came off of my life," she says. "I panicked when I heard that Sales Directors have to make a speech. There are two things that I knew I never wanted to do: fly on airplanes and give speeches.

"It's hard to believe now, looking back, but when someone told me that only the top 10 nationally have to speak, I committed right then to making sure that I always stayed out of the top 10. That way I could have a business I enjoyed without having to speak or fly on airplanes. I told myself, 'I'm just a simple east Texas girl who is not capable of doing either. So I'm just not going to do it.'"

But Dingler's life script was already being rewritten. Her new coauthors included the women she had recruited into the company, who wanted her to go to the top. They included her husband, who, as she says, "saw Mary Kay as a real personal growth opportunity for me." It was he who figured out a way to overcome Dingler's fear of flying. He asked a pilot friend to take her into the cockpit of an airplane and explain everything. They included her best friend and Mary Kay colleague, Senior National Sales Director Nan Stroud, who showed up the first time Dingler had to make a speech and many times thereafter.

As Dingler sees it, those coauthors included Mary Kay Ash herself. "For many thousands of us," she explains, "Mary Kay believed in us before we could believe in ourselves. She saw success for us before *we* could see it. She had the wonderful ability to 'praise people to success.' "

Dingler recalls vividly the watershed moment in her career. One day in 1969 a special-delivery letter arrived from Mary Kay Ash, asking her to share her success story with the entire sales force at the Seminar. It was no easy task—her husband had to take a week's vacation to calm her down and then drive her to Dallas—but she ultimately rose to the occasion. She has never looked back since.

The subsequent milestones in her career came in rapid succession. She decided to become a National Sales Director because, as she recalls, "I saw a particular pink Cadillac model that I wanted and was told that model was available only to National Sales Directors."

She became the number one Independent National Sales Director in the nation only after her Area Sales Directors came to her with a plan. They wanted to go for the top spot and wanted her to help take them there. Again, Dingler's story underscores the importance of colleagues who serve as the coauthors of a new life script.

"It is amazing to me how much it has meant to me to occupy the number one position," she says today after being number one again in 2002, "especially when you consider that I spent a good bit of my career shunning the top!"

But there's no doubt in her mind as to what changed her thinking. In fact, she can point to the specific conversation that set her on the course for the top. "When I finished my speech that day in 1969," she recalls, "Mary Kay walked up and said it was a great speech. It had an enormous impact on me. And that's one thing that Mary Kay did so well with all of us. She showed us how to stretch ourselves, achieve our goals, and then how to coach others to greatness. I see now that being a great leader takes the ability to encourage others and to constantly challenge them to do what they think they cannot do."

Of course, it was proven success that earned Doretha Dingler her unwanted place on that stage in 1969. But even as she rose to speak, she still believed in her heart that she shouldn't be there and couldn't succeed in that new role. The warm reception she received and the pat on the back from the founder herself caused a profound rewriting of her life script.

As Dingler puts it, "I said to myself, 'Maybe I *do* have something to offer.'"

OK Never Does It: You've Got to Be Great

Managers who allow their employees only to maintain a level of mediocrity inevitably lead mediocre companies.

Conversely, managers who insist that OK is simply not enough tend to lead great companies.

But this difference doesn't come about by accident; you have to consciously commit to being great. You have to commit to challenging the people around you in constructive ways so that they live up to their potential and constantly revise upward their estimation of that potential.

I recently saw an interesting television commercial that featured children ostensibly looking ahead into their careers.

"My life's ambition," one said, "is to work at a company until I'm in my forties, so I can be downsized."

"I want to work at a company, retire, and get a gold watch when I'm turned out to pasture," rejoined another.

It was both funny and sad. The point obviously was that the world of business is often not too encouraging and that people are all too often the victims of mediocrity and mismanagement.

When people and organizations commit to become great, they can travel the road to excellence. They can help each other rewrite their life scripts. The leaders of Mary Kay Inc. have made this commitment. In interview after interview I encountered an extraordinary degree of enthusiasm. Almost everyone I talked with had a story to tell about how someone challenged him or her to commit to achieving extraordinary results. No one—literally no one—expressed the willingness to just be OK. Most people wanted, and expected, to be *great*.

SECTION III

CONCLUSION

12

The Golden Rule and Mary Kay's Leadership Practices

We were an equal opportunity company long before it was fashionable.

—INDEPENDENT SENIOR NATIONAL SALES DIRECTOR
ROSA JACKSON

OVER THE YEARS a number of scholars and businesses have studied Mary Kay Inc. Frequently they're interested in the highly visible aspects of the company: the pink Cadillacs and so on.

Few have studied what I think is one of the most interesting aspects of the company. What happens when a company that for many years has had the benefit of an extraordinary leader—the founder and inspiration of the enterprise—loses that leader? What steps, if any, were taken in preparation for that inevitable moment? And how effective have those steps proved in the subsequent months and years?

In the last chapter I described how Mary Kay Ash, as far back as the early 1970s, began training leaders in the independent sales force to serve as her motivational stand-ins. Over time this effort has proved highly successful.

When Mary Kay Ash suffered a debilitating stroke in 1996, the challenge to the company intensified. The senior leadership team decided that it had to find a way to ensure that the overall approach of the firm did not change, even as the founding generation was leaving the scene. This was not a sentimental or nostalgic decision, of course—far from it. The members of the executive team, many of whom had experience at other large companies, recognized and valued the differences in the way that Mary Kay Inc. did business. They believed that the success of the company derived in large part from those differences. Ensuring the company's future success inevitably became linked to identifying and sustaining those differentiating practices.

This chapter is about those practices and how they became codified and instilled in the entire company.

Darrell Overcash, Executive Vice President of Global Human Resources and Operations, offers some thoughts on the human dynamic of Mary Kay's leadership:

> *Mary Kay clearly and fervently believed people were born good regardless of how external factors may have influenced their lives. Inherent in that belief is that we are all basically good people who want to do what is right. She realized that any of us could be victims of our surroundings but that no matter where we are in life, we can change. Her theory was, "It's not where you start, it's where you finish." It is evident to me that what set Mary Kay apart as a leader is that she saw through to the core of human nature. She looked beyond all the external factors to find the real person. Add to that her ability to breathe belief into people and you begin to understand her genius.*
>
> *What we've observed in human resources is that people who connect with our culture want to stay. Let me hasten to add that existing within this culture includes focused effort, hard work, and numerous challenges. These are givens around here, just as in any other competitive business environment. And we're not perfect. We make mistakes.*
>
> *We do strive daily to strike the delicate balance that is at the heart of the Mary Kay priorities. God first, family second, and career third not only requires belief in these priorities, it requires a strong work ethic and a strong commitment. Mary Kay Ash had a strong work ethic, and for some reason many*

people miss that part of her story. What we've found is that hav-
ing a strong work ethic is an important part of the equation to
create balance in your life. We truly believe that finding this
balance is as equally important to our success as are the efforts
to be profitable. Some would argue that it is more important.

The "Practice Rules"

Over the years, Mary Kay Inc. faced tough decisions, large and small.
When it came to the large decisions, the founder was almost always
involved. But when it came to the smaller decisions, when Mary Kay Ash
was not likely to be consulted, people often invoked the ideas of the
founder.

That was not particularly hard to do. Many of her trenchant observations were already part of the oral lore. "Do the right thing," someone
inevitably would say when a tough ethical decision was being confronted,
invoking the founder's guidance. And of course Mary Kay Ash wrote a
number of books—including her autobiography and *Mary Kay on People
Management*—that provided additional guidance.

These things were helpful, of course, but it is difficult to run a fast-
growing corporation on the basis of anecdotes and autobiography. The
company's leaders therefore decided that they wanted to take the essence
of those Mary Kay beliefs and boil them down into clear statements of
leadership.

The result of this collaborative effort is the Mary Kay Leadership
Practice Rules. These 10 rules reflected how Mary Kay conducted herself
as a manager and summarize how she wanted others to lead. Once
adopted by the executive team, these rules were published and used as a
guide for leadership practices at the firm:

Mary Kay Inc.
LEADERSHIP PRACTICE RULES[1]
*Employee commitment to an organization is founded on trust
and is a reflection of its leaders' decision-making process, people management practices, and communication style.*

All Company leaders, from first-line supervisors to members of the Executive Team, can directly contribute to strengthening the bond between employees and Mary Kay by consistently doing the following:

- *Always do what is right, honorable, and ethical.*
- *Always consider the human impact of every decision before a final decision is made. Use the Golden Rule as a guide for determining the right thing to do.*
- *Before doing something, always consider, "How will it appear to employees and affect employee morale?" Make sure it's the right thing to do. If it is, and it may be perceived negatively, explain it to employees before doing it.*
- *Before doing something, ask yourself, "Will it impact on employee trust?" Make building employee trust and confidence a top personal priority. Morale is every leader's responsibility.*
- *"Speak" to employees, don't "market" to them. Effective communication is open, frequent, and timely, in good times and bad.*
- *Allow employees to do their jobs. Reduce bureaucracy where possible and empower employees to make decisions. Measure employees' performance by "their batting average, not their last time at bat."*
- *Each time you interact with employees, sincerely demonstrate that you respect, value, and appreciate them. Be approachable, open, and honest.*
- *Think before taking action or making a decision. A "knee-jerk" reaction to a problem or situation may not be the right decision and can erode employee respect for the decision makers.*
- *Remember that employees are real people with diverse backgrounds and multidimensional lives. Value their personal differences, recognize their individual circumstances, and respect the whole person that each truly is.*

- *Always strive to be fair. When in doubt, err in favor of the employee.*

This simple one-page summary of leadership rules is currently the standard for leadership behavior at Mary Kay Inc. and is the focus of all the leadership training at the firm.

Perhaps your reaction to the above is "nice but not realistic." Perhaps you are surprised at the lack of specificity in light of its purported importance to the running of a major company. If so, I suggest you put these rules to the following test.

Make a number of copies of the practice rules and distribute them to a group of friends who work at different companies. Ask them to read the practice rules and answer the following questions. Ask them to answer each question by using a five-point scale, as follows:

1 = Strongly disagree
2 = Disagree
3 = No opinion
4 = Agree
5 = Strongly agree

Statement 1: The Leadership Practice Rules clearly reveal how I would like to be treated as an employee. Answer _____

Statement 2: The Leadership Practice Rules are in accordance with how I am treated by my current employer. Answer _____

Statement 3: At a company where the Leadership Practice Rules are used by management to lead others, the company will be more profitable. Answer _____

Statement 4: Very few companies manage their employees with this approach. Answer _____

Statement 5: Organizations where employees are treated in accordance with these rules would have more talented people applying to work there than would companies that do not use these rules. Answer _____

As I was working on this chapter, I conducted an unscientific survey using this brief questionnaire. My goal was to see if the Mary Kay Leadership Practice Rules would pass muster with the kinds of people they were designed for, but outside the organization that spawned them. My respondents came from a variety of companies—many of them Fortune 500 firms—in a range of different industries. A majority of those polled held middle to senior management positions with their companies. Here are the results:

- There was unanimous agreement among the respondents that the rules described how they wanted to be treated. This is a great lesson for aspiring managers.
- More than 80 percent of the respondents replied that they are not treated in the manner described in these rules. I find this interesting because although the rules set a high standard, I don't believe it's an unattainable standard or even close to that. It's mainly an issue of commitment, and if my respondents are to be believed, only one in five companies today behaves the way that 100 percent of people want it to behave.
- Some 70 percent of the respondents believed that companies that applied the rules would be more profitable than those that did not.
- Nine out of ten respondents believed that most companies do not manage their employees with the approach described in the Mary Kay Inc. rules. I guess the silver lining for corporations in this is that although there are a lot of unhappy people out there, they don't necessarily see greener pastures elsewhere.
- Over 90 percent of the respondents believed that companies that applied the rules would have a larger talent pool to choose from than would those that did not. Well, that's interesting. If great people make great organizations, don't organizations have to invest in the things that appeal to great people?

To say the least, my informal survey suggests that the opportunity exists for most companies to make a dramatic improvement in the way their leaders lead. Unfortunately, many corporations are now going in the opposite direction. They seek to invest less in their leaders and, by extension, in their employees. Instead, they opt for the "-ings": downsizing and outsourcing. And they do so in ways that directly contravene the letter and spirit of the Mary Kay rules.

Where Mary Kay's Leadership Mattered

"Value differences." "Be fair."

These two statements are generalities, but when they are applied consistently across a corporation, they can be quite powerful. They can be especially powerful when they run against the grain of either an industry or a society.

Rosa Jackson, who began her Mary Kay business in 1969, helps make this point. Jackson and her husband lived in Atlanta at that time. He was completing seminary studies, and she was studying for a master's degree in religious education. An African American, she was invited by a white friend, another minister's wife, to attend a Mary Kay skin care class.

Jackson immediately saw an opportunity for herself with a Mary Kay business. She and her husband were barely surviving as he went through the seminary, but he was so convinced that this was a great opportunity that he borrowed $250 to buy inventory. Jackson's business soon met with success, and naturally enough, a lot of her friends decided that they wanted to start their own businesses.

Then prejudice reared its ugly head: A number of people in the Atlanta area let it be known that they didn't think Mary Kay Inc. should have a "black" face. "And that's when Mary Kay personally got involved," Jackson recalls. "She became my personal cheering section. I will never forget what she said to me, and remember that this was way back in 1969. She said, 'Rosa, I apologize for our society. I believe we are all equal in the sight of God. You can go to the top in this company, so don't let a few narrow people discourage you.' Over the years Mary Kay was always there for me."

With the company's strong backing, the looming obstacles in front of Jackson disappeared, and she was free to build her business. Today she is an Independent Senior National Sales Director with four "offspring"

National Sales Directors in her area, including the first African-American woman to achieve that distinction.

Value differences. Be fair.   Because of Mary Kay's lifelong belief in equality and because of the company's commitment to embodying those values, the Mary Kay independent sales force today includes more than 88,000 African-American women and more than 94,000 Hispanic women. Together, these two groups make up almost 28 percent of the current U.S. independent sales force and help ensure that the company is represented in the widest possible range of communities.

Ruell Cone's story shares some of these elements. The firm was 13 years old when Cone became the number one Independent Sales Director, breaking all previous company records with $700,000 in unit retail production. She was the first African-American Independent Sales Director to break into the top 10; she was the first to achieve the position of Independent National Sales Director.

Cone is the daughter of sharecroppers. At the time she joined Mary Kay, she and her family owned two trundle beds (in which the entire family slept), a refrigerator, and a piano. That was about it. During her Mary Kay career, while a single mother, Ruell was able to put her three children through medical school and build a dream life with her business. Cone believes strongly in the Mary Kay commitment to creating opportunity for anyone who is willing to work hard and prove herself.

At the other end of the spectrum from Jackson and Cone is a third African American who has had many opportunities in her life but who nevertheless believes that the Mary Kay opportunity is among the best. She is Independent National Sales Director Gloria Mayfield Banks, who discovered that a Mary Kay business could provide her with flexibility and a lifestyle she was unable to find in the corporate world. Banks has a master of business administration (MBA) degree from Harvard, and today she is one of 10 African-American women who have achieved this career pinnacle in the Mary Kay independent sales force.

The company has 13 women with Hispanic roots who have become National Sales Directors, not including the late Independent National Sales Director Maria Elena Alvarez, who was the first in 1991. Thirty years earlier, at age 13, she had been airlifted out of Fidel Castro's Cuba.

The most successful woman among the Hispanic sales force today also fled political turmoil in her homeland. Independent Senior National Sales Director Nydia Payan is a native of Nicaragua. The recipient of a college scholarship to Italy, Payan was called home by her father's illness and subsequent death. After marrying and starting a family, Payan worked alongside her husband to make a better life. When her country began to be wracked by civil war, she started to look for a way out.

First, she sent two of her three sons to the United States. Then, in 1979, the entire family was reunited in the United States. With her sister's encouragement, Payan began a Mary Kay business two years after arriving in the United States. By 1998 she had achieved the status of National Sales Director, and she is currently a member of the Inner Circle.

Lily Orellana also emigrated to the United States, in her case from El Salvador. Her story is another one that involves the overcoming of great obstacles. Orellana cleaned houses for three years in the early 1980s. In 1984, while taking night classes with her husband to learn English, Orellana met a Mary Kay Independent Sales Director. She soon began her Mary Kay business and by 1990 was living a version of the American dream. An Independent National Sales Director since 2001, Lily today owns the kind of house she formerly cleaned. "My greatest thrill," she says, "is watching the women in my area improve their lives and gain confidence to become better women, wives, and mothers."

I cite these stories at some length because in an anecdotal way they validate the results of my informal survey cited above. People believe that valuing differences and being fair is good business, that it makes a company stronger. These stories substantiate that belief. Mary Kay Inc. has the benefit of the kinds of outstanding performers just described because it embraces diversity and extends opportunity on an equal basis. It does this because it is the right thing to do (and Mary Kay Ash always said, "Do the right thing."). But it also does it because doing so is good business.

Great Leaders Are Great Teachers

Great leaders are usually great teachers who create other great teachers around them. Just as Mary Kay Ash had a profound impact on Rosa Jackson's life, Jackson has touched thousands of lives as a mentor, coach, and teacher. Those who understand leadership recognize the difference between telling and coaching. It's walking the walk, not merely talking the talk.

There are certainly some situations in which a top-down, micro-managing autocrat, focused on all the details and barking out orders, is exactly the right prescription for a company. For example, it may be what's needed to pull a company out of a tailspin. But in the vast majority of cases what's needed is less of an autocrat and more of a coach. In the corporate context, as in the sports world, coaches teach. They teach a code of conduct, a philosophy of leadership, and sometimes even a way of looking at the world. They build people up and lead by their own example. And in the case of a great leader that example is *memorable* and *powerful*. It is leveraged because people who have been affected by it want to share it with others.

Leaders are teachers. There is a saying, "Give a man a fish, and you feed him for a day; teach him to fish, and you feed him for a lifetime." The same is true of leadership. Telling someone what to do is of no long-term benefit to the individual. Teaching someone how to do something can benefit that person for the rest of his or her life.

Independent Executive National Sales Director Anne Newbury had the opportunity to work alongside Mary Kay for nearly 30 years. "She understood leadership, and she understood how important it was that she teach us how to lead," says Newbury. "I think the first lesson we learned was the 'stretch' lesson. Mary Kay knew how to get you to set extraordinary objectives; then she would coach you on how to achieve them."

Newbury recalls many times when Mary Kay would challenge someone to reach for a goal that seemed impossible. She personally experienced that moment when, after receiving an award at the Seminar, she walked past Mary Kay Ash. The founder leaned forward and whispered something to the effect of "Next year it's going to be higher. There's nothing more wilted than a laurel sat upon."

Newbury also saw Mary Kay coach people to excellence. At one Seminar Mary Kay was talking about setting exceptional goals. The discussion centered on a very high goal that someone was going to attempt to achieve within six months. Mary Kay reminded the individual of how most people go about achieving a goal like that. "Most people will procrastinate for five months and three weeks," she said, "and then they will get busy and hit their goal with a week of real effort. Why not just cut out the five months and three weeks of procrastination and get the job done in one week?"

If you have ever managed a group of salespeople, you know how insightful these observations were. Not only have most of us seen others procrastinate for five months and three weeks on such a goal, we have done the same thing ourselves. And note that Mary Kay was not only getting her people to set extraordinary goals, she was offering suggestions on how to achieve them.

Much of what Mary Kay taught people focused on coaching others to excellence. Newbury tells how Mary Kay often would talk about people (leaders, in this case) as being one of two types: "basement people" or "balcony people." Basement people are those who keep you down, whereas balcony people are those who lift you up and cheer you on. Mary Kay believed that it was impossible to coach unless you were a balcony person. She lifted others up and then showed them how to do the same thing.

Earlier in the book I discussed the self-limiting way in which most people view themselves. They describe themselves in terms of what they *cannot* do. The unbounded view, by contrast, focuses on all the gifts, abilities, and talents a person has and all the things a person *can* do. According to Newbury, coaching is all about getting people to discover the unrealized abilities they have.

Newbury explicitly equates her job as an Independent Executive Sales Director at Mary Kay with that of a coach. With career earnings in excess of $7 million, it would be easy for her to sit back, rest on her laurels, and count her money. She doesn't do that because she takes her coaching role too seriously to permit any self-indulgence.

"My give-back," says Newbury, "is to 'coach up' others so that they can climb the ladder of achievement just like we did. We say, 'I'm going to stay on your case until you succeed.' And we *do*."

One of the reasons there is turnover in the direct-selling business is that a certain percentage of would-be salespeople enter the field with the mistaken impression that it's an easy road to riches. But high achievers such as Anne Newbury emphasize that there's no free lunch in the direct-selling business. "The people who succeed in this business are committed to excellence and hard work," she says. "There is no substitute for that."

Newbury also carries that philosophy over into her coaching. She is the first to say that success involves giving up some things. In order to "have it all," Anne believes you have to learn to make appropriate sacrifices, and that includes carving out the time needed for success in business. "I'll call some of my team at 5:00 a.m.," she says. Of course, she is quick to add, she has their permission to ring at such an early hour. "I want them to understand that champions are disciplined people, and if you have a family you want to take care of, you have to be creative about making the time to be successful."

Mary Kay Ash loved challenging the sales force to join what she called her "Five O'Clock Club." She had discovered she could add an extra working day to the week by getting up an hour earlier each day.

Today Newbury feels she can spot someone who is going to be successful early on. "I'm always looking for that person who says, 'I'm in,' " says Anne. She discovered one of those special people just a few years ago. "This woman made the commitment to let me coach her," says Anne. "She never questioned my guidance, and today, just a few short years later, she's a National Sales Director and a member of the Inner Circle."

Coaching leadership, in other words, *does* work. It not only helps build a successful organization, it also is a path to personal satisfaction. Newbury explains that one of the real joys in her life today is getting to watch someone else achieve success. "The money that's attached to success is nice," she elaborates, "but the real reward is when you get to see others discovering that they can do great things. It's all about bringing someone up."

In 1971, when she lived in Massachusetts, Newbury got a call from an executive at a Boston securities firm. It was an old, well-established company that enjoyed a good reputation in the securities industry. The executive had become interested in finding out more about this company in Dallas called Mary Kay Inc. He had gone to the phone book to see if he could find a listing for the company, and there he found Anne Newbury's name as a Mary Kay independent sales force member.

The executive invited Anne to lunch with him and his associates at the firm. They had never met a real-live Mary Kay Beauty Consultant and wanted to know more about the company and how it worked. The team was fascinated as Anne described the practices of the firm. For her part, Newbury could see that the securities firm was a slow-moving, bureaucratic organization, and she was convinced that the firm could benefit from adopting some of the approaches used at Mary Kay.

"Oh, that Mary Kay stuff would never work in a male world," responded one of the executives with a hint of condescension in his voice.

Newbury chuckles as she recounts that story. "Well, it sure looks like a lot of companies are trying to emulate our practices *now*," she says.

"Let the record speak for itself. We're a $2.5 billion company today; that's quite an accomplishment when you consider it was a $5,000 investment in 1963."

Theory MK Leadership

Many academics and consultants have become celebrated for developing a theory of management that gains widespread acceptance. Douglas MacGregor, for example, made waves with his ideas about Theory X and Theory Y management. There are countless others as well as a whole host of motivational schemes.

There is one thing, unfortunately, that most of those theories have in common: They talk a lot *about* leadership and management, but few of them speak about the *hows* of leadership and management.

That is why I suggest that the business world consider embracing what might be called Theory MK leadership—in other words, a conceptual scheme that addresses the "hows" of leadership.

Theory MK is about *getting things done*. It's about *making things happen*. As Mary Kay Ash often said, "Some people watch things happen, some people wonder what happened, and some people make things happen." It is an active, interventionist, optimistic style, one that looks for and praises the good in people and then harnesses that good for both individual and corporate gain.

Note

1. Used with permission of Mary Kay Inc.

13

Walk the Talk . . . All the Way to Russia

IN THIS FINAL chapter I want to offer a few concluding observations about the company I've had the privilege of studying over the last several years. But first, in the spirit of Mary Kay "storytelling," let me include another brief Mary Kay Inc. success story. Although some of the details are surprising, the basic outline of the story is consistent with what you've read in the rest of the book.

More Than a Harvard MBA

Every year Harvard Business School professors invite executives from selected companies to visit a class to discuss their companies. On one particular day Professor Robert Simons had invited Dick Bartlett, vice chairman of Mary Kay Inc., to speak to the class.

Harvard students are expected to be insightful, analytical, and comprehensive in their approach to looking at companies. Part of the class is devoted to students' comments about the company to the guest executive. And on this day one student had come to the conclusion that Mary Kay Inc. was not a very good company.

As Bartlett recalls it, the student started by criticizing the marketing approach of the company, which Bartlett headed at the time, and then dissected the company's strategy, disapproving of every detail. Finally, he delivered his conclusion: "There really isn't much future for this company."

Bartlett, very much surprised, listened as the student plowed ahead with his aggressively negative analysis: "This is simply not a good business model. It's just a bunch of housewives selling cosmetics. The recognition systems are inadequate, and the strategy is unsustainable. How could a company like this be successful?"

It was then that another member of the audience—an African-American woman and a member of the Harvard staff who happened to be sitting in on the class—stood up. Her name was Gloria Mayfield Banks.

"Let me tell you a few things," she said. "I have a Harvard MBA, and I've worked my way up through the corporate world. Now I'm back here working at the Harvard Business School as the assistant director of admissions, and I happen to spend my evenings selling Mary Kay cosmetics." She went on to explain to the student that he simply did not understand a central fact: Many women viewed the "Mary Kay opportunity" as one of the best around. "Most people," she added, "simply do not understand the opportunity that exists at this company."

Telling her personal story to the class, Banks made it clear that she understood that opportunity from firsthand experience. Having graduated a little more than a decade earlier from the Harvard Business School, Gloria took a position in manufacturing with Polaroid. After two years with that company she took a sales position with IBM Corporation, selling large computer systems. Then, four years into her new career, she was advised that it was time for her to "move up" into a higher position in the company. She turned it down. The problem with the new position was not only that she would have to take a considerable pay cut—she had been earning substantial commissions—but also that there would be no way for her to affect her income as she could in sales. "It simply made no sense," recalls Banks. "Why would I take on more responsibility, work even longer hours, for a lot less money?"

Banks then accepted a position as a marketing manager at a major computer manufacturing company. During that time she went to a friend's house for a Mary Kay skin-care class. "I didn't even give her enough time to ask me if I wanted to become involved in selling the product," says Banks. "I walked up and asked her how I could sign up. I immediately saw the opportunity with Mary Kay."

For the next few months Banks held down her corporate job during the daytime and at night took care of her children while also working on her Mary Kay career. She qualified for the use of a career car just five months after she began her business. (The career car is one of the first major awards a Beauty Consultant can receive.) She continued to pursue her Mary Kay business when she later returned to work at Harvard University. One day, she heard that a Harvard Business School class was going to discuss Mary Kay Inc., and she asked Professor Simons if she could sit in.

According to Dick Bartlett, when Gloria Mayfield Banks finished explaining just how great she thought the Mary Kay career was, the classroom was dead silent. Finally, Professor Simons broke the silence. "It seems to me," he said, "that Gloria is on a path to making more money than many of you in this classroom today."

That's not quite the end of the story. After a little more than two years at Harvard, driving a pink Cadillac and enjoying a Mary Kay income substantially higher than her salary at Harvard, Banks felt that she could no longer justify holding on to her "day job," and so she resigned her position to pursue a full-time Mary Kay business.

She has earned the use of a pink Cadillac for the last 12 years, broken company records, and earned the position of Independent National Sales Director. During a phone conversation with Gloria, I commented on all the phones ringing in her office. "Well," she said pleasantly, "I run a $16 million company out of my home. That's why you hear all the phones ringing."

When asked about her personal keys to success, Banks responds that it all hinges on finding people who want to achieve more in their lives. "It can involve someone who wants to improve her appearance," she explains, "or someone who simply wants to have a great career and still be able to spend quality time with her children. You show me someone who has a dream to get better, and you have found a winner."

The Future: An International Company

But what of that Harvard Business School student's comments that there "isn't much future" for Mary Kay Inc.?

As was noted earlier, the company does have to worry about eventual penetration of the domestic marketplace. (No company grows at double-digit rates indefinitely.) If for no other reason, Mary Kay Inc. has to take steps to build a strong international presence and get solid footholds in parts of the world that may constitute strong markets in the future.

This work is well under way. Mary Kay's first overseas subsidiary was established in Australia in 1971, and over the ensuing 30 years or so the company and its independent sales organization have worked together to discover how to create a global future. In addition to the 180 U.S. National Sales Directors as of 2002, there are currently 80 Independent National Sales Directors in the international markets.

Perhaps one of the most telling hints of the international potential Mary Kay has in international markets came in April 2002, when the *New York Times* wrote about a Russian woman whose life was transformed by the company. The headline read: "Russian Rights Crusader, Made by Mary Kay." Anya Vanina is no longer an Independent Beauty Consultant, but she says the lessons she learned continue to affect not only her life but that of her entire community. "The company's teachings—financial independence, international sisterhood, and lifestyle—appealed," the *Times* article says. And in Vanina's own words: "That American company made a revolution in my life. It exudes a tender care and value for people that amazed me."

Russia is Mary Kay's best-performing market in Europe, and it has had high initial growth since it began there in 1993. Mary Kay Inc. came to the former Soviet Union in the wake of perestroika and glasnost, according to Tara Eustace, vice president of the company's Eastern

Europe operations. Women throughout Russia and all 15 now-independent Soviet Republics have, according to Eustace, triumphed in their Mary Kay businesses "through civil wars, lack of heat, electricity, and running water." They have overcome the absence of workable transportation and services as well as the lack of a strong middle class. What's even more amazing is that according to Eustace, the average monthly wage in Russia is $100. And even though a Mary Kay basic set costs $65, women are willing to make this investment and are finding the customers to justify that investment. There are now more than 30,000 Independent Beauty Consultants in Russia, and the market is already nearing a dozen Independent National Sales Directors.

The first National Sales Director in Russia, Galina Kisseleva, holds advanced degrees as an engineer-ecologist. She worked at the Mendeleev University of Chemical Technology in industrial ecology before setting up her Mary Kay business. She recalls that when she first heard about Mary Kay, "it sounded to me like a fairy tale." After a trip to Dallas, where she met Mary Kay Ash, she was sold on the company. Then she met a group of Russian immigrants who were Independent Beauty Consultants living in New York. "You cannot even imagine," they told her enthusiastically, "what a future is waiting for you!"

Today Kisseleva describes the company as one with "a vast future, a company that has a place for everyone who is full of desire to bring knowledge, beauty, and joy to others." She says Mary Kay not only helped her change her life but also "gave a new future to my children to see a new philosophy of work."

Across the ocean, in a vastly different context, is Mary Kay Inc.'s number one market after the United States: Mexico. Again, given the relative lack of disposable income, this might strike some people as surprising. And yet, says Mary Kay Latin America President José Smeke, "The culture of our business fits a major need in the country."

But that's not because the Mary Kay culture has been modified in significant ways to conform to Mexico's needs. The "fit," Smeke says, was already there: "Our business culture and principles are things that we don't need to twist or reinvent for our markets. Mary Kay teaches women not only how to dream but, more important, how to *achieve* their dreams."

Guadalupe "Pipis" Castro Mendoza is a great illustration of what Smeke means. Left by her husband when their child was barely two years old, Mendoza had no car, no home, and no extra money when she started her Mary Kay business in 1991. She cooked food to sell in her town to make ends meet.

"I had no desire to continue living, and my self-esteem was very low," says the Independent National Sales Director, who claims she has been "living a miracle" since 1992, when she became an Independent Sales Director with 76 team members and more than 400 basic customers: "Since then everything has been like a dream." Mendoza recalls that it was a calculator offered as a prize that first sparked her interest, but what kept her going were weekly telephone calls from her Independent Sales Director. "She would ask me, 'How are you?' and I would answer her with 'Fine,' although I was embarrassed to say that. After a while I began to believe it."

Guadalupe recalls the pride she felt in 1997 when her son, then eight, spoke at her National Sales Director debut. Considering all that they endured together, she calls it her favorite Mary Kay memory.

Smeke says that Mexico's tremendous growth as a subsidiary market has come primarily since 1997 and has seen the Independent Beauty Consultant count climb from 12,000 to 100,000. Today there are almost 1,400 Sales Directors in Mexico, and retail sales in 2001 were $100 million at wholesale, which represents $200 million at retail.

Another star in the Mary Kay constellation is the Asia-Pacific region, where countries from Korea to Australia are working to "paint the world pink," says K. K. Chua, president of Mary Kay Asia-Pacific.

"This region is one of the most diverse in terms of political systems, religious affiliations, and cultural practices," says Chua. "And yet the Mary Kay 'way' has thrived."

In China, a land of 1.4 billion people, more than 68,000 women have Mary Kay businesses in 40 cities throughout the country. "The self-esteem of these women," Chua says, "the fun of what they are doing, and the practice of Go Give and the Golden Rule are all thriving in this socialist state."

Gu Mei, the first Independent National Sales Director in China, was also the first pink car driver in her country. She recalls a four-year odyssey that took her from dreaming to achieving. She had no money to purchase luggage, and so she walked to her skin-care classes carrying bags full of her products, with one showcase on her arm and another on her shoulder. "I did this every time I held a skin-care class," she recalls, "and that was more than 12 times a week. My shoulders were always black and blue."

Mei recalls hearing about the pink Cadillac from an American Sales Director, and so she regaled her guests at every class with the idea that in America women earned pink Cadillacs. In 2000 she was honored as the first "pink Santana" driver when China's car program began. (The Santana is the domestic Chinese equivalent of the Cadillac.) Comments Mei, "It was then I knew that this dream, which I never doubted, had come true."

I've focused on Russia, Mexico, and China because they illustrate the range of countries that are now proving to be fertile markets for Mary Kay Inc. As of the writing of the book, the company has 33 active markets. With some obvious exceptions—for example, countries that place active restrictions on the kinds of activities that women can engage in or restrict contact with the West—there are very few political or economic impediments standing in Mary Kay Inc.'s way. It appears that the "formula" is applicable worldwide, with some tailoring to reflect local conditions and needs. No matter if it's a pink Cadillac or a pink Santana: It captures the same spirit worldwide.

That's why Dick Bartlett was so surprised to learn up at Harvard that he had hitched his wagon to a company with "no future." From his perspective, things look quite different.

Going for the Distance

What does it take for a company to endure and prosper for a century or more?

A number of people have attempted to answer this question, including Jim Collins in his book *Built to Last*. It turns out that there's no simple answer. Great product quality alone won't do it. Committing to excellence alone won't do it. Strong values or a powerful and positive organizational culture alone won't do it. A lot of great companies that have excelled in one or in some cases several of these competencies have failed to thrive.

Sustainable success requires the ability to do a lot of different things well. Early in this book I offered a definition of management: the leading of organizational learning, transformation, and performance. What that means is that sustainable performance is driven by *leaders* rather than by managers obsessed with detail. It also means that the company is always in the process of learning about the future and then changing to adapt for high performance.

In Chapters 3 through 11 I introduced what I called the "Nine Keys" to high organizational performance. They are as follows:

1. Create and maintain a common bond
2. Shape the future (think and act strategically)
3. Make me feel important (value people)
4. Motivate others with recognition and celebration
5. Never leave your values
6. Innovate or evaporate
7. Foster balance: God, family, career
8. Have a higher purpose
9. You've got to be great (exceptional excellence is the only acceptable goal)

Companies that last 100 years or more generally exhibit all of the nine keys. As I have tired to demonstrate in these chapters, the subject of my study—Mary Kay Inc.—has the benefit of all nine. (This shouldn't be surprising, since it was during my research at Mary Kay Inc. that these keys came into sharper focus.) Today the company's challenge is to build on this foundation and move into the future.

Not surprisingly, Mary Kay Inc. has its own list of priorities for the future. In a recent conversation, David Holl, president and chief operating officer, told me how he viewed the company's direction:

> *There are at least four factors that will determine our future:*
> *First, we have to never become so big that we forget where*
> *we came from. Mary Kay Ash used to say that "becoming a very*

big company and managing to act like a small company" should be our goal. As we approach 1 million independent sales force members on five continents, it's increasingly important for us to focus on how we invest in and manage the business.

Second, we have to focus on further penetrating our existing markets. As our founder was fond of reminding everyone, "Nothing happens until somebody sells something." We know that a devoted sales force and a loyal customer base will keep our market shares growing in the United States. Direct selling and cosmetics are industries we understand and can continue to build upon.

Third, we need to take advantage of the giant strides in technology while at the same time transforming a cold, impersonal tool into a friendly medium of communication. When we look at our technology advances of the past five years, we know we must continue to invest in projects, systems, and customer service tools that will maintain our sharp focus. Mary Kay Ash spoke about how we should always "sandwich criticism between two thick layers of praise." I have a take on that. We should always sandwich our technology between two thick layers of warmth and caring so that any independent sales force member can have trust and a comfort level about how Mary Kay's technology-based initiatives can help achieve her business goals. We must provide the tools that relate to her needs and make her life easier.

And finally, in responsible and respectful ways, we must continue the work to spread Mary Kay's dream worldwide. We have gained an awareness that international expansion works best for us with our own formula of "doing it right" rather than rushing. We know that common goals are sometimes best reached by going down different avenues; every market, every sales force member, and every employee is unique.

In his conversation with me Holl mentioned a favorite quote of Mary Kay Ash from Thomas Jefferson, who once said, "In matters of principle, stand like a rock; in matters of taste, swim with the current." And if I had to point to a single factor in the past successes of this company—and its best prospects for the future—I'd point to its rocklike quality.

Mary Kay Ash, her personal belief system, and her company all have an air of timelessness to them. Just when they start sounding a little, well, old-fashioned, you are surprised at how contemporary or forward-looking they actually are. Does Mary Kay Inc. speak more effectively to—and for—American women of the era in 1963?

Or does it speak more effectively to and for the women of Russia, Mexico, and China in the early twenty-first century?

My point is that when you adopt as your mission statement something as fundamental as creating opportunities for women, you are very likely to find that your mission, and therefore your market potential, is virtually limitless.

I'll give Mary Kay Ash the last word. (In this case she was speaking to her independent sales force leaders in 1995.) In the age of Enron, WorldCom, and so on, I invite you to savor a worldview that began to be forged in a dying Texas town way back when the automobile was still a novelty and may well represent a voice of the future:

> "We need leaders who add value to the people and the organization they lead; who work for the benefit of others and not just for their own personal gain; who inspire and motivate rather than intimidate and manipulate; who live with people to know their problems and live with God in order to solve them; and who follow a moral compass that points in the right direction regardless of the trends."

Index

Jim Underwood, Ph.D., is an award-winning author and business professor. He has been a strategy consultant to many international organizations and has written five books on the topics of leadership and corporate strategy. He lives in Irving, Texas.